AVERAGE SUCKS

WHY YOU DON'T GET WHAT YOU WANT

(And What To Do About It)

MICHAEL BERNOFF

An imprint of
Srishti Publishers & Distributors

Srishti Publishers & Distributors
A unit of AJR Publishing LLP
212A, Peacock Lane
Shahpur Jat, New Delhi – 110 049
editorial@srishtipublishers.com

First Published in India by Bold,
an imprint of Srishti Publishers & Distributors in 2023

First published by Scribe Media in 2020

Arranged via Licensor's Agent: DropCap Inc.

10 9 8 7 6

Printed and bound in India

For Sale in India Only

This book is dedicated to my wife, Debra, for your unwavering love and support of this mission and book, which serves as an example for our daughters Tara and Maya to always live an above-average life.

CONTENTS

INTRODUCTION

I'll never forget the feeling in my stomach when I saw the varsity hockey roster, and my name wasn't on it.

I can still smell that mix of sweat and ice at the rink as I searched the list for my name again...and again, double-checking myself just in case those awful fluorescent lights were playing tricks on my eyes.

This had to be a mistake. Obviously this was a mistake.

Except it wasn't.

The coaches felt I just wasn't good enough for varsity.

I played it cool but inside I was mortified. If there was a way I could have melted into the walls I would have, but nope, I had to look at my friends that did make the team and say "Congrats, man, good job," and keep my shit together. I made it through the bus ride home, but once I walked in my front door, I let loose. I got angry, I was throwing things, shedding tears—all because I didn't make the varsity hockey team.

I was so confused. Hockey was my thing! I loved hockey as a kid, playing every chance I could get ice time, begging my dad to drive me to the rink at all kinds of odd hours. I played street hockey when I couldn't get on the ice and I worked my butt off to get good, and I was pretty decent. I felt I was just as good as many of the guys that did make the team and there was no way I could understand what happened. I stared at my ceiling all night trying to make sense of it and just got angrier with every tick of the clock.

Eventually I cooled off long enough to go talk to the coaches, and they were honest: they thought I could be a really good player, and that I was basically good enough to play varsity, but that I was totally underperforming my potential. They thought I was holding back and hesitant. Since I was only a freshman, they wanted to give me the motivation to really improve and come back next year really ready.

That was all I needed to hear. My strategy to get on the

varsity team was to work hard, and so I did. That was what my parents always taught me. Work hard and push hard if you want to be great.

I spent the next year working harder than I'd ever worked, pushing myself past my old limits, and doing "all the right things." I trained as hard as anybody else. I worked as hard. I went to all the right clinics. I practiced endlessly to get better.

And I did get better. The next year I even made the varsity. And I played on the varsity for three years, until I graduated.

But as cool as that was for me, the reality is: I was still pretty average. I worked really hard, but I got average results for my entire varsity hockey career. I never excelled. If you saw the effort I was putting in, you would've thought I'd be way better than I was.

There isn't a happy ending here.

I was just an average high school hockey player.

The most painful part is that *I should have been really good at hockey*. I had everything I needed to be a really good hockey player. I was 6′6″. I was a good athlete. I was tough. I had good hands. I could even skate well.

But, I was just average.

I made a lot of good plays on the ice, but I never scored goals, and as a forward, well, that was how my position was judged—by goal scoring.

So I never made any fancy travel teams or all-star teams. And because of this, I never moved on to play college hockey, or anything more than that. The idea of that never even occurred to me because it wasn't something I thought was possible for me. Never even hit my radar.

I promise this is not a story about some guy who can't get past his high school glory days (this is a story that's about you, and you'll see why in a second).

Fast-forward twenty years. I'm way past my physical prime, but I play in a men's hockey league. Many of the guys in my league played at some collegiate or professional level. They are really good players, even better than the kids I played against back in high school.

The high school me would have been intimidated in this league...but I'm not because in this league I'm really good. I score two to three goals a game on average.

And I've been doing that for three years.

Understand—even playing against average goalies, it is really hard to score a goal in hockey. To get two or three a game consistently is almost unheard of.

But I do it. Now, I'm a sniper. I got two goals again this morning. I just pick the shot I want, and I get a few in the net almost every game.

How did this happen? How did I go from being just average in high school, to being a very good player twenty years later on the dad's league where the only girls we're talking about in the locker room are our cute little daughters?

Did I go into an intense hockey training regimen? Maybe I really dug in, practiced and trained, and sharpened those skills I didn't work on in high school?

Be serious. Not even close. I haven't practiced hockey on any real basis since high school.

OK, then it had to be a serious strength training and fitness regime, plus a nutritional plan, maybe some other neat tricks of expensive trainers that turned me into a physical machine?

Come on. I like occasional sweets and sushi way too

much, and I pick up weights here and there, yet nothing like hitting the gym in high school.

In fact, there is only ONE thing that changed in my whole body, and that has made all the difference:

My mindset.

You see, what happens in your life either confirms who you are, or it changes you. And I finally got my moment and stopped confirming, and started changing.

Here's how it worked:

When I first started playing in men's leagues, I still just showed up as an average player. I did a solid job, was a fun person, played average. I wasn't remarkable on the ice in any way—I was just one of the guys that came out on Thursday nights; sometimes we'd win and sometimes not. Back then I would score a goal once a season (maybe).

Then one day I thought to myself, "How come I don't score goals?"

I asked myself the same kind of questions I would ask my clients to help them work through business problems, finance problems, or relationship issues. I had this conversation with myself:

New Michael: “How come I don’t score goals?”

Old Michael: “Well, I’ve never been a goal scorer before.”

New Michael: “Well, why not?”

Old Michael: “I guess I never actually attempted to be one.”

New Michael: “Well, are you good enough to be a goal scorer?”

Old Michael: “Yeah, I think so.”

New Michael: “Well, dude—what if you started trying to be a goal scorer? What would happen then?”

Old Michael: “I don’t know. I’m not sure I know how to be a goal scorer. I’ve never done it before.”

New Michael: “Well...what if you pretended to be Jack?”

Old Michael: “I could do that. Let’s give it a try.”

OK, this Jack was a kid I went to hockey camp with, who was the best goal scorer I ever played with. Now he was a remarkable player. He was magic. It was so easy for him to put that puck in the net and I remember being in complete awe; it seemed like every time he took a shot, it went in.

So the next shift, I literally pretended to be Jack. I thought the way I thought he would think, moved the way I thought he would move and acted the way I thought he would act.

And I scored a goal.

> Old Michael: "Interesting."
>
> New Michael: "See! You ARE a goal scorer!"

I scored a goal on the next shift as well. And over the next few weeks, as I continued to play like Jack, I realized that goal-scorers were doing one thing I never did.

I was only concerned about shooting the puck. They were concerned about the puck crossing the goal line.

I was shooting the puck. They're shooting the puck. I was getting as many shots as they were.

But they put the puck in the net. And I didn't.

So I focused on that—getting the puck across the line.

And I kept scoring. Within a few weeks, I didn't need to pretend to be Jack anymore, because I'd adopted my own new identity:

Michael Bernoff, goal scorer.

What's so funny is that my skating never got that much better. My stick handling barely got any better. I didn't even become a great hockey player. Nothing changed with my skills. I am not a better hockey player than I was five years ago.

The only thing that changed was *how I perceived my identity.*

Before, I almost wouldn't let myself score, because it wasn't my identity. It was beyond My Average.

Then, I decided to become a person who scores goals.

There's a happy ending to my hockey story: a few years ago my wife sent me to the USA Hockey Team Miracle on Ice Fantasy Camp for my birthday. Basically, it's where older guys pay a ridiculous amount of money to play with the guys from the 1980 Olympic Miracle on Ice team (maybe you saw the Disney movie made about their story).

And at the first game I got the MVP.

All it took to make me a consistent goal-scorer in my men's league and the MVP at the Team USA Fantasy Camp was shifting my mindset from being "not a guy who scores goals" to being "a guy who scores goals." I had all the talent and skills I needed, I just had to believe that I was that guy, and then make the mental shift.

Sounds easy, doesn't it?

If I wanted to beat myself up about it, I could definitely point out how ridiculous I'd been, because I could've done this years ago.

It took me years to see it in my own life, even though this is what I help people do for a living. I teach people how to change a few words or adjust the way they see things and change their life.

That's literally what I do.

I know, I know—I'm the cobbler whose kids have holes in their shoes.

Even though I've helped tens of thousands of people level up in their lives, I've always just had a story in my head that I'm average. I grew up thinking I'm probably the most average person on earth (outside of my height). I've always just put myself in the average box. I never wanted to put myself out there. Even with hockey, I just told myself I will play with these guys and be average and be happy with that.

After I became a goal-scorer, I asked myself—what else am I telling myself a story about?

Where else am I average, only because I tell myself that I am?

It's been a major exploration of my life, and has helped me level up in so many ways.

And it's what led to this book.

Even though people had been asking me to write a book for years, I didn't do it because unconsciously I told myself, "Average people don't write books."

I've helped tens of thousands of people change their finances, or build a huge business, or create an amazing marriage, or become incredible parents using these techniques, so why can't I put them in a book?

Of course I can.

And this book is the result of that realization:

Anyone—including you—can change their average and become who they want to be.

This book will change how you communicate with yourself. All life is held in the context of communication. Relationships, health, business, money, all of it is hinged on your ability to effectively communicate.

The core message of this book is that you can communicate with yourself differently, and in a way that raises you to a new level.

You can break out of your old average and raise yourself to a new level, and that is what I'm going to teach you.

I'm not average.

Neither are you.

Literally all you have to do is simply change your perspective, and possibly a few words in your head, and you can do exactly what I did, and become the person you want to be.

WHAT DOES ANY OF THIS MEAN TO YOU?

OK, hold on a minute: what does some middle-aged guy scoring goals in the dad's league have to do with you?

How is that going to make your life better?

Well, nothing I teach in this book is about hockey. Hockey

is just how it became glaringly obvious to me in my life. It's the vehicle that taught me about how the concept of average is the key to real, lasting self-improvement.

But before I explain how averages control your life, let's think about your life. Ask yourself some questions:

Do you ever feel held back?

Do you feel something you can't explain that's keeping you from moving forward?

Do you feel like you're capable of more?

What about your relationships? Are they good enough? Do you want to show up in them in a better, more engaged, more connected way and get that same feeling back?

Do you ever feel like you're having trouble being yourself?

Do you feel, instead of creating your life, you're just accepting what comes your way?

Maybe your life isn't even that bad. Maybe nothing is wrong, really.

You just know things can be better.

You're not who you want to be. Yet.

You might be looking for answers, but can't seem to find any.

Maybe you feel stuck. Bored. Not fully alive.

Do you ever just say to yourself, "I thought there'd be more to life?"

Or you ever say to yourself, "I'm doing OK, but I'm not who I want to be yet."

If any of that is true, then this book is for you. In fact, you are the exact person I wrote this book for:

The person who knows they can do more, but doesn't know how to get what they want out of life.

WHO IS MICHAEL BERNOFF ANYWAY?

OK, so who am I anyway? Why listen to me?

It's a good question. I won't bore you with a long bio, but I will tell you how I got into the business of helping people create real and lasting change in their lives. I started my career when I was a kid, mowing lawns for money in the summer, which then turned into a summer landscaping business—which turned me into an entrepreneur.

In college, I got involved in direct sales, worked really hard at it and—not trying to brag—I killed it. Until I didn't, I hit a wall and that's when, at nineteen years old, someone handed me a book and told me it would help. I read it and for the first time in my life I realized that I could learn how to influence my life. It was a complete shift from what I'd always known; work hard and it'll pay off.

I became obsessed with the idea that you can influence your life through the power of communication and soaked up all the information I could on communication, selling, persuading and making more money. I soon started coaching other people in my company to improve their results, too. During those years it became really clear to me...I loved helping people. It was much more fulfilling for me to watch someone else get really good at closing a sale, using something I taught them, then closing a sale myself.

Little by little I coached people until I was able to make my dreams a reality and within a few short years, I turned my obsession into my passion and then it became my mission. I spent every free moment diving even deeper into human psychology, language patterns, beliefs, behavior, and motivation, and used it to assist people in transforming their lives, going past their limits, and raising their Average, quickly.

As I worked with people, I realized that I had a very unique ability to connect and move people using the power of communication. My clients were getting life-changing results and I was becoming more in demand.

Knowing I was on the right path, I founded the Human Communications Institute.

Since then, I've helped 100,000's of people through events and seminars, and have worked directly with thousands of people from over thirty-five countries. I'm a highly paid consultant to C-level executives and business owners, I work with well-known professional athletes on performance, and I coach celebrities and influencers on how to be better at, well, influencing.

I do this because I am passionate about making a difference and changing the world, and I know the best way for me to do it is through my programs and by teaching people to change their lives through communication.

More importantly, I am committed to teaching people strategies to influence their own lives.

I believe we all have the capacity for greatness, and I want to help as many as I can—including you—get there.

WHAT THIS BOOK WILL GET YOU

I won't make wild promises. This book is not a magic pill or a cure-all.

I've been teaching what's in this book for the last fifteen years, and I've seen the changes that happen in people when they finally "get it" and make the shift.

The first thing that usually happens is that people realize they're not alone. They see that this is a real problem, and that lots of other people share it.

Then they realize there's a solution. That other people have suffered from this, and found their way through it, and they can actually do something.

The next step tends to be action. People actually start understanding how their average is impacting their lives, and they start shifting how they think and feel.

This action usually creates results.

Their lives change. Whether it's scoring more goals in their hockey league, or being more confident in relationships, or starting a business, or anything—the point is, action creates results, which creates more actions.

Once they start to see results, they tend to feel like they're more in control of their life. Which helps them start facing some of the lies and half-truths and bullshit in their lives. And they get the tools to change the things they want to improve.

Which of course creates a positive whirlwind—the more you face your truth, the more you use your tools to create change, and the more control you feel, the better results you get, etc., etc.

This then tends to lead to something really profound: self-acceptance.

People stop beating themselves up. They accept who they really are. They're finally OK with who they are, and the things they do.

The final step tends to be a new identity. This new identity allows people to finally show up as themselves. To stop holding back. To show up in their relationships for real. To have the courage to be themselves.

They raise their average, they settle in and are happy... and then the process begins again.

This is the missing piece with almost all personal development: once you raise your game, what do you do then? How do you move to the next level?

In this case, you repeat the process.

Forever. Because life has no finish line. You can always get better, and this is the process you can use to do it, forever.

WHAT EXACTLY WILL YOU LEARN?

OK, this all sounds great. But how exactly is this book going to help you get there?

I'm going to introduce you to a new framing of the concept of "Average." In short, this is what I'll show you:

1. You have an average.
2. Why you have this average.
3. What your average means.
4. How your current average keeps you from getting what you want.
5. How you can get what you want by accepting you have an average, and then using it to raise your average.

It sounds simple. And once I explain it, it will seem simple.

But it's not easy to execute.

In fact, I would say that really implementing the ideas in this book, if you do it right, will be some of the hardest work you've ever done on yourself.

But it doesn't have to take forever, it can actually be quick.

And if you're willing to work hard, what's great is that it's not complicated. It just requires determination, and effort (and the guidance you'll get here, in this book).

Let me be clear:

This book will not immediately fix your relationships. It won't make you more money tomorrow. It won't get you in shape just by reading the words.

This book will not make you feel better right away.

If anything, about halfway through the book, you're going to feel worse because you're going to become really aware of the truth of your life. And that truth won't be super pleasant at first.

It is not a self-help book you can read and not take action on. If you don't want to take action, if you just want to read something that will make you feel good without having to do anything, then you might not want to read this book.

It's not a book you can casually flip through and look for the numbered list of things to do. There are no scripts to memorize.

It's simply you opening your eyes to Your Average and doing the work to raise it.

This is a book meant to change your life, but it requires commitment on your part.

Let's get started.

CHAPTER 1

PUTTING A LABEL ON YOUR PROBLEM

I get stopped a lot by people in the street. Not because I'm attractive or famous (not even close).

No, I get stopped because people agree that "Average Sucks."

I have a license plate that says, "Average Sucks." I have shirts I wear all the time that say, "Average Sucks." And people love it.

The response I get is always the same, "That is so cool man. You're right, dude. Average does suck. To hell with average, you know, I never want to be average."

It's typically somebody doing well. Somebody pretty proud of their life. And so I ask them, "Do you have any idea what it means?"

And they respond, "Oh yeah. Being average sucks. Most people are average, and I'm not. And my whole goal in life is to be above average."

And that's when I tell them, "Not at all. That's not what it means."

And they get just as confused as you probably are right now.

SO WHY DOES AVERAGE REALLY SUCK?

What Average Sucks means is something very different, something much deeper. Understanding it is the answer to the question, "How do I get what I want in this world?"

To put it plainly: Average Sucks is all about moving past YOUR average, so that you can become who you want to be.

So why does Average Suck? Well let me ask you this first.

Have you ever had the feeling you're capable of more?

You know how sometimes you get that gnawing feeling that you could be doing so much more with your life?

It may be hard to explain, and you may not want to admit it to others, but when you are alone and you're looking back at your day or your month or whatever part of your life—you know there's a whole other level you haven't reached yet. You feel it and you know it.

You should be playing at a higher level.

Even if other people perceive you as "doing great," even at this very moment you may actually be kicking ass, doing so much better than you were a few short years ago—it still never feels like enough.

There's still a piece of you that feels like you're a bit of a loser if you don't push harder.

On one hand, you're proud of all you've done. On the other hand, your inner voice is saying, "I know I'm better than this, there has to be a better way. What am I missing?"

You know if you can just get to that next level, then you'll be more fulfilled.

I've had these thoughts and feelings my entire life.

I had this sense that these feelings were important and were there to let me know I was special, yet I didn't understand what to do with them.

Now when I talked to a few people I really respect, I realized they have the exact same feeling and it is just as hard for any of them to explain it with words.

The best way I can describe it is like I have this driving force inside of me, this feeling that I am truly special in this world. We all are, right? Most of us believe we are uniquely special in our own way. Well I'd even go so far as to say that I believe I've got something special inside me that other people don't have.

I say that humbly yet with certainty that I know I am meant to do great things, and when I follow that gut instinct and push myself and take action on my ideas, it's like that force inside me gets stronger and stronger. And that's how I know I'm right. And that's how I know I'm not meant to be average.

You see, when you do more and when you do better, you feel even more powerful and confident. And the more you do those things the stronger that invisible force gets, guiding you and driving you to do better, to be better in any area of life. And that's when you feel invincible and truly alive.

But sometimes, sometimes I'd feel that force sending me in a direction...yet when I got there, or closer to where I wanted to be, something was stopping me. I'd literally run into a wall and there was no way I could go around it, over it, through it...nothing.

This feeling Sucks! That's the feeling of your average holding you back. That's the invisible, deflating feeling you get anytime you're going for something new and you stop. It's super frustrating and hard to identify, even though everyone feels it. Welcome to your average.

If you were to scream "Average Sucks" at this very moment, you would be correct. You would be yelling at the actual feeling that holds you back from either doing something new, or succeeding at something you have never done before. It's the feeling that keeps you where you are. Sometimes, it's the fear from doing something new, and other times it's motivation to not lose what you have.

But what on earth is it?

Well, it's "Your Average" and that is what's holding you back.

YOUR AVERAGE CONTROLS YOU

I'll give you an example. I live in Arizona and here, the mortgage and real estate business is huge. I know many people in that business, and I've seen them now go through three different economies. What's so crazy is that almost all of them literally make the same amount of money.

Good economy? They make 300 grand.

Bad economy? They make about 275 grand.

Good economy again? They make around 325 grand.

There's no common sense reasoning why people make virtually the same amount of money in totally different economies...other than they have an average. Your Average controls who you are.

I talk to people all the time about "Your Average." And they think I am saying that they are an average person.

But I'm not. I'm saying they have an average, and it controls who they are.

I have a friend who we'll call Drew, who in every way imaginable was successful. He successfully ran a publicly traded company, was happily married to his beautiful wife, had great kids, pets, houses, cars, health, travel, fun...you name it he had it, he was well Above Average. And really, he didn't have to bust out of his average if he didn't want to, because his average was giving him a really amazing life. Yet one day when we were talking, he told me he'd really like to be able to be a better presenter. He was frequently in front of large crowds, and did OK, yet he knew he could do better and wanted to feel more comfortable and also to be more engaging. What he didn't realize was he was at the end of his average and wanted to raise it. So that's what we worked on; he learned how to simply talk and share instead of attempting to present perfectly and he learned how to use language patterns that captivate the crowd. I've seen him speak several times since then and it's clear that his average has gone up considerably. Improving his life in this one area improved his total average and his entire life is better because of it!

I tell you that story because I want to make sure you get this, it's very important. When I say your average, I literally mean "Your Average" as in "the average that is yours." We all have an average that we tend to be at most times.

I do NOT mean "your average" as in "you are average." If I was saying that, I would spell it that way.

Now listen carefully, that is *not* what I'm saying.

This is NOT about comparing Your Average to anyone else's. It's not, I'm better at this, he's better at that, I do this well, she doesn't. Throw that idea out of your head right now. That way of thinking is a guaranteed recipe for a miserable life. Drew wanted to be a better public speaker because he knew he was capable of it, not because he was trying to be like someone else.

Nothing in this book is about comparison to anyone at all...except yourself.

EVERYONE HAS AN AVERAGE

Who does? You do.

Everything and everyone in this world has an average. I have an average. So does Bill Gates. Unless he makes a specific type of effort to change and follows through on it, his average will control his actions and he'll end up the same person at the end of the year.

Baseball players have a batting average, the Dow Jones is an average, your intelligence is measured by your grade point average...everything in life has an average. Your average determines how well your life works.

Your Average makes your life give you basically the same thing year in, year out.

So think of Your Average like this:

Your Average is the invisible wall that stops you from doing what you want to do, saying what you want to say and being who you want to be.

And this is the thing stopping you from getting what it is you want in this world. And the only way to grow as a person, to reach a new level and become who you want, is to first recognize and accept you have an average and then transcend Your Average.

Obviously there's not a physical wall. It's just a feeling that stops you harder and faster than any wall and it's so powerful you don't even try to get past it, because Your Average says you can't. It unconsciously stops you from even attempting.

You know how alcoholics must first accept they have a problem before they can fix their problem?

It's the same thing with Your Average.

To figure out your current average, you absolutely must acknowledge that you walk around with this feeling that you're not quite good enough to go for the next big thing, whatever that is to you. You must acknowledge that something unconscious in your mind stops you and you're not even aware of it.

I know that feeling well, I've had it so many times in my life. Believe me, *nobody* wants to admit it out loud, yet I'm certain that you know the feeling well. It's the feeling you have when you must own a mistake, or when you go for a goal and don't reach it, or when you want to speak up and you don't, and the moment passes and you're stuck with your silence.

I've already talked about my high school hockey days of not being good enough...and when I think back to how My Average came about, I can pinpoint specific times I remember getting "that look" from my coach when I'd mess up a play and although I can't describe it, the feeling is so familiar and vivid I can think of it right now and feel it if I wanted to. It was in those moments that My Average was created and I accepted it.

And that sucks.

And a lot of people accept average and live that way. And that sucks as well.

Yet you, you're reading this book and just like me, you have that invisible force driving you to find a way past the wall. And you can.

Because here's the deal, being average my entire life meant I was not a gifted athlete, not a great student, not recognized as anything special and definitely not the most successful...and that *bothered* me. I hated it.

And so I would push. Mostly I'd push to be the most likable, to have the most friends, to make the most money, to have the best of whatever was important at the time. And then when I became an adult I wanted even more things...money and health and love and success. All of it.

Pay attention.

Your ambition is running around with Your Average like they're best friends...and not getting anywhere.

My mom used to tell me not to be friends with certain kids I grew up with because they were a bad influence. That makes sense, especially now that I'm a parent and want my girls to select great friends. You want good influences in your life. Yet here you are as an adult letting Your Average be a bad influence on your ambition and holding you back.

Now for me, the problem of My Average showed up in my consistency. After years of attempting to figure out exactly what was stopping me, I came to realize my inconsistency was my weak spot. I wanted to be successful but

My Average caused me to stop too soon, fall short and, although I'm embarrassed to admit it, give up.

Welcome to the roller coaster. I'd get excited, feel the driving force, start over and go crazy, hit the wall, stop, feel average. Start over, hit the wall, start over, hit the wall.

I was being controlled by My Average, and I didn't even know it.

WHAT IS YOUR AVERAGE?

OK so you get it, you're controlled by Your Average. But how did you get there?

It was a mystery for me for years, why I couldn't get ahead—Once I changed it, my life and my clients' lives transformed almost immediately.

Let me tell you about the day My Average first went down. That day started like any other: I woke up, ate breakfast, and headed off to summer camp with a group of friends I'd known the majority of my short life. Once there, I must have looked lost because a counselor asked me, "Michael, are you looking for something to do? Why don't you go play in the sandbox? It looks like those kids are having fun."

Like any five-year-old I shrugged. Why not? Sand, kids, fun? I'm in!

I walked up to the sandbox and said, "Hi, can I play with you guys?"

The response was positive, so I sat down in the sand with the other children. A couple of seconds later I heard a loud CRACK and felt a sharp pain as a kid named Andrew smacked me on the side of the head with a toy car, the General Lee from *The Dukes of Hazzard*. Whether intentional or accidental, I'll never know. Either way, it hurt and tears ran down my face in pain and embarrassment.

I'd never had anybody hurt me before and it was so painful, both physically and emotionally, that I knew I never wanted that to happen again.

It was at that very moment my brain kicked into gear, doing its security and protection job, and took note of what happened and wrote a program to make sure that never happened again. It built a plan without me even realizing it that said, "avoid these types of situations."

My little five-year-old self learned a lesson that day; walking up to a group of people you don't know is a scary thing, and it can be downright dangerous. Proceed with caution.

Even though I never thought about that day much ever again my mind would never forget the lesson. It is crazy what shapes us and yes, all events will shape you. In my case, a General Lee changed me and molded me, without my permission, into a person that was cautious in new situations. And it did it under the guise it was going to protect me.

So the protection program was installed and shaped my new Average and Identity and for years since that day any time I had to walk into a new circumstance—whether showing up to the first day of school or walking into a birthday party—I'd get a weird feeling inside. I wasn't a shy kid, exactly, but I definitely held back in a lot of areas of my life. When I called a girl to invite her to a dance, it took me forty-five minutes to dial six out of the seven numbers. Then another thirty minutes of nonsense talk until I could get to the point. Even in my early years in business, cold calling and talking to people I didn't know made me incredibly uncomfortable.

At the time I didn't understand what it was, and I figured that everybody felt the same nervousness as I did so I'd better find a way to get as comfortable with being uncomfortable as I could. I had no idea what I was really doing to myself.

So if we were talking face-to-face I bet the question you'd ask me right now is "So, what is My Average?"

Your Average is you.

Let's take a closer look at that...When people think about what's holding them back they'll refer to it as fear, fear of the unknown...or maybe they feel like their past is holding them back. I've even heard people call it a "fear of success" which is total bullshit. I've heard all kinds of descriptions; some ridiculous, most nonsense.

For most people, it feels like resistance. It's that feeling you get when you're standing at the edge of a diving board for the first time. Should I jump? Should I climb back down the ladder? All you have to do is jump but for some reason you stand there immobilized, a force stopping you from jumping. There's nothing there, yet you can feel it as if you were tethered to the ladder.

I want you to focus on the way you are feeling right now. Are you getting irritated? I hope so. Hopefully you are getting this...you must get this or just stop and reread this section until you do, because it won't work until you get it. Your Average is you.

Your Average controls your primary thinking and your actions and behaviors.

Hopefully you're realizing how average you've been and how much you've been holding back—and feel ready to bust out of it. Hopefully you're also remembering the miserable feeling of Your Average pop up as you read this and it's making you feel committed to resolving it. Permanently.

Because the truth is not pretty, but here it is:

If you think you are fooling people, you aren't.

If you think that on the outside it looks like you're doing great and people only see what you want them to see, you're wrong.

If you are holding back, playing small and settling... people know it.

Maybe you can fool some people but you can't fool everyone, especially the people closest to you. And when you look at yourself in the mirror and face your biggest critic there's no way you can fool yourself.

Realizing this is a very powerful step in getting you out of your current average. Understand that the people closest to you can see what you're capable of and watch you not doing anything about it...sucks.

Being Average Sucks and you can't hide from it.

And I will now ask you, just like I ask all of my clients, one of the most important questions you will ever be asked in your life.

IS THIS HOW YOU WANT YOUR STORY TO END?

Your Average Sucks and if you keep going the way you're going, this will be how your story ends. Are you OK with that? I always say that on my gravestone I want it to say "Michael Bernoff, Did It All" and I mean that. Where I am now is not how I want my story to end and I know you don't either.

I've been lucky enough in life to have people that care about me hold my feet to the fire. I've loved myself enough to own My Average and go for more. And I've had to get mad at myself and say NO MORE SETTLING to break out of My Average. Now it's your turn.

The reality is, we have a standard for what it is that we do, and we have trouble breaking past that. Even if you want to, you don't. You may even be smart enough to ask people to help you, or you read information that gives you a new idea, and you kind of get past it for a small amount of time only to wind up back where you started.

Let's get right in there and talk about money: How much has your income increased over the past few years? I'm guessing you're making almost the same amount of money each year. Maybe you have some incremental growth, but nothing to write home about. I bet there are years that you made the same amount and it actually makes no sense, especially doing all the work you did. You should make more when you've been at it longer, right?

But instead your income flatlined. And when you factor in the economy and inflation and real estate market increases, it actually ends up looking like you're making less.

Why would anyone settle for that? You don't want that, do you?

What most people do is they look for hacks to get goals. You're picking up average information to solve an average problem, but all that gets you to do is take average action.

There you are being who you are, taking average action, attempting to solve this problem and you don't have a name for it, playing your situation over and over again with frustration, looking for answers to solve your avarageness.

And nothing happens.

You're acting like Your Average.

If this frustrates you, it's because you've not accepted Your Average. You may be frustrated because you feel like you've worked so hard and it should have paid off by now.

I've heard it before, I get it. When I first start coaching with my clients, their first reaction is to explain and defend themselves, "But I've done this, I've got that title, I've accomplished this, that and the other," etc.

People want to validate what they're currently doing with examples of their personal accomplishments that are superior to the masses. I already said this is not about comparing yourself to others. This is about you comparing your current self to the you that you can be. It's so predictable, we're human after all and we want to tally up all the things we're doing right in defense of what we're not doing and as a distraction technique.

Every time someone tries to convince me of how great they are, I ask that same question I asked you earlier, "Is that good enough, is this how you want your story to end?"

Because if that's good enough for you, we can stop talking right now.

I certainly don't want to waste my time trying to convince someone to raise their average. Just like me in hockey, at the time I accepted My Average and stopped, getting mad at the coaches and blaming them for My Average. How many times do people take their own below average behaviors and blame it on people or events or situations?

I understand now that I was blaming my coaches back in high school yet it was really all on me, and if I tracked them down today I'd apologize for my behavior and thank them for not accepting My Average.

So are you ready to take ownership of Your Average?

You must accept you are not where you want to be.

WHAT'S WRONG WITH YOUR AVERAGE?

Everything is wrong with it, if in fact you do want more.

OK, so here's where you're at right now:

You've settled into Your Average, and it's not *all bad*. There's actually some good to that...what it does is allows your life to be easy, allows your life to be automatic. Take a breather.

By itself, this is actually not a problem. There is nothing socially or morally wrong with settling into Your Average.

But if you want more from your life, you can't do that.

It is impossible to get what you want if Your Average controls what you do, because it will just keep you where you are.

That's what this book is for: people that have accepted that what they're doing up to now is OK...but they really desire and are capable of more. They aren't necessarily upset with their place in life...but they thought they'd have done more by now.

Do you understand that Your Average is your dominating force designed to make your life easy? You've got to remember your brain wants your life to be easier. It wants to keep things in automatic.

This is why diets are hard for people. I've worked with so many clients over the years that want me to help them lose weight. They actually don't even care if they're all that healthy, they just want to drop pounds. I know this because they are fixated on some ridiculous diet plan that they think will work. They're called fad diets for a reason.

I had a lady named Trixie come to one of my events and all she could think about was this extra hundred and some odd pounds she was carrying around. I remember her raising her hand and saying she was having a challenge with losing weight and wanted to know could I help her?

I flat out told her no. She wasn't ready and I knew it.

I listened to her language and watched her mannerisms as she talked and could easily see her entire identity was wrapped up in needing to lose weight.

Her Average was an overweight woman and there's not a diet or an exercise program in the world that will change Your Average.

Don't get me wrong, she can temporarily lose weight. She can force herself to eat healthy and exercise and hate every minute of it, and that's what will happen because that's Her Average.

But until she changes Her Average, she will fail miserably at every diet she tries.

You see, when you go on a diet, your body has an average. It's got an average weight, body composition, muscle mass, everything. It's got an average of how often you work out. It's got an average of how you feel about your body. Everything is associated with a very specific average that you calculated years ago, whether you realize it or not.

And the reason I call it an invisible challenge is you don't even know it's there. You did this to yourself for a very specific reason. Change Your Average and you'll become a person that chooses differently.

Which is exactly what Trixie did and dropped all the extra weight, started doing activities outside with her sons and completely changed the amount of joy she was having in her life.

Let's get real...a person with a high Average doesn't force themselves to eat healthy, it's what they do naturally. A person with a higher Average doesn't dread going for a run, they get off on it. Living healthy is who they are—they are their average.

So now do you get why all your diet plans have failed?

So now do you get why you aren't consistently exercising?

Every single thing you do in life is programmed and monitored by Your Average.

Now here's the part where people get confused. Because along with the times they didn't follow through on things in their life, they are remembering every single time they worked hard to make something happen.

Why is Your Average running based off of your weakest behaviors, instead of creating an average from all the times you've made an effort? What about all the times you "were good" and ate a salad instead of a burger? That doesn't seem fair, does it?

I get it. I hear this all the time because we're all humans and again, just as I said in the very beginning of this book, our brains are looking to validate what we're doing. Our brains want us to feel better about ourselves.

Look, Your Average is not your weakest behavior, Your Average is your most common behavior which is most often your weakest behavior.

Understand, the message in our brains of who we are was also designed in an instant and reinforced over time by you without you consciously knowing it and the truth is Your Average wants you to stay the same because that's the program it's been given. It likes things just the way they are. If you stay the same, then you won't take a risk and you won't get hurt. So the goal of Your Average is to keep you safe and certain of the next step.

Now as I'm saying this to you, I'm reminding myself of the areas I need to raise My Average. Because everything I'm saying to you applies to me, too.

Literally, this book is the perfect example of how My Average had me stuck for years.

Because I'd been thinking about writing this book for ten years. TEN YEARS!

I knew the concept, but I didn't have a name. Then one day my daughter's cheerleading team was performing at a competition, and halfway through their three-minute routine, technology failed and the music cut out.

But they kept going without stopping.

They gave the exact same routine anyway, without music and ended the routine with "zero deductions," which in cheerleading world is everything.

I was blown away watching them...they were absolutely incredible!

Then it hit me. This is what they've trained for all season. This is what I've been paying for as a parent, getting them so skilled and confident and prepared that they can do their routine no matter what.

It hit me in that moment, I realized right then and there that this was their average!

I was standing there watching these smiling girls, so proud of themselves for nailing a routine with a perfect score despite the challenge and it hit me: Average Sucks.

Now why would I say Average Sucks after telling you about that winning performance?

Are you getting it?

Because that Average got them to a great place. In fact they took a trophy during that competition. Their average kept them safe, made them perform at a level. It did exactly what it was designed to do.

That's the concept that hit me in the midst of all those shrill teen girl screams. People get to a point that they are proud of and then they get stuck. And that's what sucks.

That's the moment I came up with the name of this book. I even wrote a note on my phone, finally putting a name to the concept that's been rolling around in my brain for years. This is what I want to explain to the world, and every person in it that can't figure out how to reach that next goal.

Because what if one of those girls were pulled off that team on the same day at the same competition and thrown into a routine on a higher level moments later, competing with girls with more skills and abilities?

Their average would kick off an automatic program without them realizing it and they'd stop saying "I got this!" and start saying "Can I do this?"

They couldn't go from doing a back handspring to a standing tuck in a matter of minutes. Sure maybe they could tough out some of the basics they already know, but if they didn't raise their average to perform at a new average, they'd screw up.

In the exact same way you choose ice cream over fruit.

In the same way you choose wine over water.

In the same way you choose sleep over jogging.

In the same way you choose talking to a happy customer instead of calling a new prospect.

In the same way you say you're making enough money but you'd really like more.

In the same way you have an OK relationship instead of a passionate one.

In the same way your bank account is what you make, spend and save and it's not enough.

In the same way you excel at what's easy for you and hope nobody notices you're playing small.

So all this time I wanted to write this book, My Average

kept telling me I'd never been a writer. I'm a speaker. I'm a consultant. I coach business owners. I coach athletes. I can train any salesperson to build rapport and close a sale without fail.

But writing? Nope, never did it.

And I also had this program running in the back of my head from elementary, high school and college that said, "Writing is hard."

As a kid, writing was the one area I had the most challenge with in school. I hated it. I hated the red marks all over my papers after my teachers read it even more. And I never broke out of that, I never got really good at writing and so that's how my story went.

So what business did I have writing a book?

I tried to write a chapter here and there of course, but it was really hard because I had never done it before. So when I sat down, immediately my brain would do every little game in its power to make certain I wasn't going to move forward.

My brain wanted me to stay in My Average. I am a speaker and—I mean this with all humility—I'm really, really great at it. I'm a coach, and when I work with people, I change their lives, I'm certain of that. I run live workshops and the results that happen for the people in the audience are incredible.

That was factored into My Average and my brain was using that to justify my greatness, justifying me not having a book, even though I wanted it!

How crazy is that?

I didn't *need* to have the book done to stay where I was.

But I did need it to level up in my life.

Here's the real, raw truth. I'm going to tell you the ugly truth of my own average right now because I want you to know that I'm right there with you, wanting MORE. Wanting BETTER. Wanting to make sure my story ends the way I want it to.

You see I was doing really well (My Average) in my business and proud of the work I was doing for people and all I'd accomplished. I've made it my life's work to teach people powerful communication that changes their lives.

Literally for every hundred people I worked with, I got through to say ninety-seven of them. If someone came to one of our events, they left happy, confident, driven and in possession of communication tools that would allow them to keep going, consistently. I'm not bragging right now, I'm just setting the scene for you.

So I had this thought in my head (My Average talking) that if I wrote a book, it would have to get through to every person that read it, or it would be a failure.

I wanted to achieve the same success rate as I had working with people live and in person.

I knew that would be impossible with a book. Especially because My Average told me I wasn't a writer. Sure, the book would reach some people, and it would get people to move in the right direction.

But could I achieve the rapid personal transformation that happens in person? I didn't think so.

That is so ridiculous!

But the real kicker came when a good friend came along and kicked me in the ass. He'd been watching me procrastinate for a couple of years and so one night he aggressively called me out on it and finally I heard something that made me push past My Average.

And here's what it was: I was OK with helping a few thousand people a year in person, knowing that I could get through to them and they could get great results and go on to live amazing lives.

But, absurdly, I was also NOT OK with thousands of people all over the world reading my book and getting *some* results, *because I knew I would only get through to some of them.*

And on top of that, my mind played all kinds of games on me that said maybe the book wouldn't be good enough.

(Of course now I realize it was My Average stopping me from my new goal and stopping me from creating a new average.)

I kept wondering how I could write into words what I did on stage, because when I'm working with people I don't have a plan or a script or know what anyone is going to say, I just roll with it and it works.

With a book, I'd have to plan it all out (I'm not a planner) and I would have to make sure I said just the right thing (I never know what I'm going to say next) and I could fail (not happening). I could embarrass myself.

I could write a bad book that made my peers not respect me.

Flat out, writing a book was a risk.

I will always remember my friend leaning across the table and looking me dead in the eyes and saying "Michael, you could be helping millions of people but you're not. If other people want to play small, that's on them. But not you. You can't be who you are and play small. You have to write this book."

So I took the risk. I busted out of My Average. And when I did that I went from my pitiful little average helping some people, to a new average (this book!) that will allow me to assist millions. And that, in my heart of hearts, is really what I want to be doing with my life.

Here's how it works:

1. Your unconscious brain avoids new things because it doesn't know what to do and wants to keep you safe. Safety is doing what you know.
2. You've gone to the outer limits of your current average.
3. You accept you're at your outer limits (Congrats!) and you realize you're about to learn something new and add excitement and challenge to your life.
4. You decide to learn how to get out of the "box" that you're currently living in and create a new and better average.

5. You take the action, do new things, get good at them and achieve a new average.

Are you ready for that?

Because I am certain that you don't want to waste time like I did stuck in your old average.

Right now, you have a choice, just like I did in writing this book.

Should I stay or should I go?

Stay stuck and Suck?

Your Average is going to theoretically attempt to sabotage every step you take. That's what I allowed it to do until the moment when my friend called me out and from that point on I shut out anything My Average had to say and I beat it, and this book is proof of it.

Now's your turn.

WHAT DO YOU DO?

If you take a look at what sports teams do to position themselves for a winning season, it's a perfect example of increasing their average. Since I'm already hockeying this book I'll use the example of the NHL Trade Deadline. Every year hockey teams have the opportunity to make final changes to their roster during regular season.

A team headed to the playoffs will willingly trade a 1st round draft pick, which is usually an on-fire, bursting with energy young player, for a seasoned player that's held the Stanley Cup over his head once or twice. They're willing to give up something that is the potential future of their organization, just to make sure their Roster Average is as high as it can be, stacked to win the NHL championship. I've watched teams trade players that have been great all year to make sure they win, and while it seems sad for the players that were about to have their chance at the cup, the team is doing what it needs to win.

That's exactly **opposite of** what most people do. You run your business a certain way, and it's gotten you this far. Why change it, if it's working? You've got a good relationship, you're happy enough, your marriage has a good flow to it. It's better than some people, right?

"The child is grown. The dream is gone. I have become comfortably numb."

Thank you, Pink Floyd for saying this so succinctly.

Comfortably Numb. Is that what you really want?

People don't want to readily stop doing things the way they've been doing them because of the work and the what-ifs. Why would you want to do more work, when it's good enough? What if the changes cause issues, like not making as much money for a while? Do you think the hockey teams have to readjust when they trade players and go through a period of transition that isn't easy? Of course they do! But they are willing to because they want to raise their average and win.

Just like you.

Now you have two ways to get there and I will show you both in this book.

One is to "grow bigger" than Your Average.

The other is to create new programs in your brain.

This book will show you both ways.

First Way: Growing Bigger. If you're feeling that you're hitting a wall, ceiling, or feel resistance in life, congratulations, you've found your new starting point.

We're going to move you from "Your Average" and bust through that invisible wall and get you to that hard to breakthrough place I like to call The End of "Your Average," and then get out of the box and on to the other side.

Remember, everyone, and I mean EVERYONE, has an average. Whether it's having a problem making another few sales each month, getting along with your kids, stopping the unnecessary pills you pop, whatever your vice may be, or on the flip side if you're a multi-millionaire and killing it in business, yet still want to reach a whole new level—still an average.

It's that famous quote from Ralph Waldo Emerson, "Unless you try to do something beyond what you have already mastered, you will never grow."

Is this how you want your story to end? Or are you simply at the end of Your Average and ready to grow bigger and push past it?

The Second Way: this way is built on you getting to your New Average by getting access to better than average information and educating yourself to create new programs in your brain.

Pep Rally? Fun, good. Average. The feeling wears off.

Seminar Junkie? Fun, good. Average. The feeling wears off.

Church Camp High? Fun, good, Average. The feeling wears off.

Shopping, a little retail therapy? Fun, good. Average. The feeling wears off.

That's all well and good and I'm not knocking anything that works, I'm simply drawing a line in the sand that says do not accept average information that doesn't create permanent consistency in your life.

You must find resources that support you as you move past the wall of Average.

And the first resource you must have is Above Average information...which you have in your hands right now. I'm not going to offer you average information throughout the pages of this book, because the challenge of the world today is that the majority of the information is average, it's outdated, and really nobody knows what they're doing out there except for very few people that can't even explain to you how they did what they're doing.

Most of the wealthy people I know, they don't know how the hell it happened for them. I've spent my life decoding what it is they do. As soon as you have above-average information, if you know how to get yourself to take the actions you need to take, that's when your life begins to change.

It's time you realize that Average Sucks.

It's about time you realize that the life you want to live is available to you and waiting for you.

You know that "Your Average" will never make you happy and fulfilled long term so it's about changing what Your Average is and becoming all of what you can be.

It's NOT about you being better than another person's average.

I fought this fact for years, I never wanted to be average compared to others. So instead I was comparing myself to myself, like "Hey, I'm better than I was, which is better than I thought I would be by now, so that's good enough, right?" Except it's not, because that is such small thinking. My Average was less than it could have been.

What if everyone changed their perspective to think that when they reached their goal they are at a new starting point? Wouldn't that create some amazing success stories?

From this point on I want you to think of your Current

Average as a starting point, and with this book you now have access to Above Average information that will equip you to grow bigger than any wall and lead you to the future you want.

CHAPTER 2

THE DEATH OF ADVERSITY

Everything in your life is either going to confirm who you are, or change you.

This is typically the part of the book where the author tells you about the tumultuous childhood they dealt with. I've already told you about the Sandbox Incident, and of course there are other stories along the way.

But I don't have a horrible story about growing up with a disability or surviving abusive parents who left me on the subway.

I don't have the other story, where my dad was a self-made billionaire and my problem was throwing money around and around overcoming an addiction to keep the family fortune.

I have a different story. With an invisible problem that you, too, may be facing and cannot see.

MY AVERAGE LIFE

I grew up very, very average.

Other than my height, I grew up an average person in an average time. I lived in a middle-class community in Rockaway, New Jersey with the most middle-class family you can imagine. I grew up right down the center of the socioeconomic class, which meant I had enough, I was OK.

"Michael," you're probably thinking, "you just said that you were OK. How is that a problem?"

The challenge with being OK is that OK is OK as long as OK is OK, and OK is still OK if OK is OK, but OK is not OK as soon as OK is not OK anymore.

Got it?

They don't make T-shirts big enough to print that sentence, which is why I simplified all of that to "Average Sucks."

The reason why "OK" really is a problem is because any time you're OK, there's no need to grow. When you grow up with a challenge, it motivates you. When you grow up rich, you have to find a way to protect all that money. But when you grow up right down the middle, you don't have to do anything.

My biggest problem was that life was a little too easy. A little too convenient.

My family had enough; we didn't need to have more. I saw my dad leave each morning and drive forty-five minutes to work at a job he didn't love so that he could support our family, invest his money and pay for vacations and college funds. My mother also worked to give us funds for those extras. Being Average at that time was great! You could save a little from your paycheck and get an interest return back from the bank that added up nicely.

Back then, you could get away with being average. If you did the right thing, you could even have an average lifestyle, which was a good one.

I saw what my parents did and thought it was wonderful. It was safe. It was easy. For years, middle-class life worked. If you worked hard enough and saved a little bit of money, you got ahead. That was my game plan, the one my parents always told me: "Be a good person, do the right thing, get ahead." It would have been easy back then to simply follow their footsteps.

The challenge was that—as I've told you—for my whole life, I've had a special feeling inside me that I have something special to offer the world, that I was capable of more.

So I didn't sign up for that plan. Because Average Sucks and I knew it then just like I know it now.

Fast-forward to today; if you're average, you're screwed. You have to be above average, right off the bat, or you're going to be in trouble. Between the food supply changing, the cost of housing and education, interest rates and the desire to buy things to make life even easier, the world has changed without the majority of the world realizing it.

So there I was, Average, and wanting to be different, not wanting to follow the same plan, but everyone around me was the same. I was surrounded by Average people and so I just did what they did, what we all did, chasing the wrong average and waiting for something big to happen. It never did...because I was being Average.

I had a wall up that I inherited that said, I'm not lower class, I'm middle class. It was my box. Just a plain average box.

FROM ADVERSITY TO AVERAGE

Want my opinion on the cause of the mental health crisis we're experiencing as a nation? The Middle Class.

- The middle class has no communal adversity.
- Confidence comes from overcoming adversity.
- Confidence comes from facing a challenge and finding a way to solve the challenge.
- Confidence comes from getting out of your box.
- No adversity causes low self-confidence. Low self-confidence, low inability to handle anxiety.
- Overload of anxiety? Mental health crisis.

What seemed like a really good idea at the time—replacing manual labor with machines, using your brain to make money, obtaining more than enough—all of that actually destroyed the problem-solving muscle that is required for people to be strong enough to get out of their box.

At the time nobody realized that Middle Class became a trap, or a box for the purposes of this book.

It's an outdated goal of a destination.

To ensure success for the next generation, we like to show our daughter, Maya, some of the movies and TV shows that we watched as kids. We watched *Little House on the*

Prairie so she could see what life used to be like before all this easy stuff came along.

Pa never said, "I'm having trouble getting to the gym." Just living on the prairie offered its own kind of adversity which was more than plenty to make him a strong man mentally, emotionally, and physically. He dealt with the weather ruining his crops, not having enough food on the table, protecting his family from the wild and losing a child...all in one episode.

Most people don't have anywhere near those types of challenges today. We're surrounded by convenience and simplicity. Want to buy something? Amazon will deliver it the next day. Want to watch a movie? Click Netflix. Even my car door opens automatically for me!

So tell me, who would have more confidence and be more resourceful? The kid who has to ride their bike to work until they make enough money to get a car, figures out how to replace the alternator when it won't start and drives the beater all through college until they get a job and can buy a new car; or the kid who gets handed a set of keys on their sixteenth birthday?

Convenience ruined our confidence.

We the people made a decision after World War II to build

an entirely new concept of living and that was the middle class. It was born from the idea that people should feel safe, secure, and comfortable. Education brought better jobs, better jobs brought better pay, better pay brought better houses and we began to work to make a nice life and to never go back to poverty again.

And it worked for a while.

Then it backfired. We became weaker as people.

For all of the world's history we'd had natural adversity around us and then all of a sudden we eliminated it. It was great, life was going well for a large percentage of the population. We didn't realize we were becoming weaker. Where once we had competition, now everyone gets a trophy. Where once we had to mow fifty lawns or babysit all summer if we wanted a yellow, waterproof Sony Walkman, now we either have it handed to us or we work a few hours at minimum wage and the newest iPhone is ours.

If we fast-forward to today, we don't have enough challenges so we create our own.

Here's a little lesson on how the brain works: The human brain loves to solve problems and is constantly searching to solve challenges. Normal survival and the natural adversity we had in the world is already handled, so now it's not uncommon to find people creating unnecessary social problems among the people around us, just to give our brains something to do. Take a look at all the harm social media is doing to the morale and confidence of teenagers of today and you'll see a prime example.

As a society, we've removed many normal challenges through progress and innovation because we want life to be easy, yet we need struggles and adversity and triumph over what life throws at us to grow.

BUILDING A BOX

It's kind of fitting that at the end of our days we go out in a box.

Not to be negative but do you realize that a majority of people spend their life in a limiting box without even realizing it?

If you don't make a change and get out of your box, you'll simply move from one box to the other without choosing what box you want to be in, and that is really sad. Whatever situations you experience form your identity and the Average of your life, until you change it.

For me the first wall of my box started coming up in the form of a toy car. I didn't dwell on the "Sandbox Incident" through the years, never really thought about it, yet it made me who I was and I was My Average. I'd identified what happened with who I was as a person. And then after that, every single time I walked into a new environment and the discomfort came, my brain would fire off a message "walking into environments you've never been in before is a risk," which would provide repetition and further confirm my "proceed with caution" average.

I must add in this point right here and now. I've told you my biggest challenge was my middle-class, average life. I've also told you that one of the things that shaped My Average at a very young age was being hit over the head with the General Lee.

As I was writing this book and talking about the Sandbox Incident to my wife, she went on eBay to see if she could find one of these toy cars. She did and ordered it to find it's literally a little plastic toy car and yes, getting hit over the head with it hurt, but compare that to the adversity of living in a log cabin with no heat in the frigid winter.

Compare that to working on a plantation for someone who didn't pay you and mistreated you day in and day out.

Compare that to living in poverty and hoping you don't get shot by a stray bullet on the way to school.

Compare that to living in a cave and waiting for your dad to kill some wild animal to be brought home where it would be cooked over a fire for dinner.

In retrospect, the General Lee was not a real challenge, it was my challenge and it's valid, yet this is the type of middle-class challenge that makes us Average.

Hear me when I say I'm not minimizing or negating your personal challenges. You may have been through hell, and if so Your Average is higher than someone who didn't. If that's you, I give you a lot of credit for getting through your struggles and I believe those are the same challenges that will make you more successful.

So you may be thinking that I'm only referring to the experiences in life that decrease Your Average. Let's be clear, your box isn't only made up of negative or traumatic experiences. It can be a joyful event that changes you for the better, like starting a business, getting married, having a baby, receiving accolades, or maybe even buying a scratch-off ticket on impulse and winning a million dollars.

The same thing that happens in your brain if you win the lottery is the same thing that happened in my brain when I got smacked by that car: a peak emotional experience.

Something new and unexpected happens in your life,

whether it's physically, mentally, or emotionally, your brain immediately starts searching for a label to put on it. Inside you say, "I've never seen this before. What does it mean?" Your brain decides that your experience was either amazing, you love it and want it to happen again, or it was horrible and you should avoid it.

You don't need to be a mathematician to figure out that Your Average is a calculation of all of the empowering and painful experiences in your life. If we only had positive experiences that raised our Average, we really wouldn't need to read a book about how Your Average Sucks. So now that the point has been made, we'll go back to getting out of the box.

At five years old, I started building walls that became my box, and I'm sure you did, too. Then you go on about your days and the reinforcements come in. The reinforcements are your life experiences that back up the story (box) you've bought into.

For me, my brain said "be careful when meeting new people" which turned me into a person who was uncomfortable walking into parties, events, weddings, etc. and a person who definitely steered clear of new relationships.

Next up, I'm seven years old and had to do the Presidential Physical Fitness Test in PE class. For some reason, somebody thought that having kids do pull-ups was a great way to prove how strong and healthy America's kids were. I'd never done a pull-up before, but getting out of math class to be in the gym seemed like a lot more fun, so I happily went along with it.

I watched the first couple of kids go up to the bar and do a pull-up or two. With a last name starting with B, I was always one of the first names called so my turn came quickly. "Michael, you're up."

So with all the confidence in the world I walked up and grabbed the bar the wrong way, with my fingers facing me. The gym teacher kindly informed me that I didn't know anything about pull-ups. "That's not how you do it." Once I turned my hands around the other way, I used all the strength in my arms and tried to pull myself up... but I couldn't do it so I hung there, my face more red from humiliation than effort. When the teacher saw that I couldn't do it, he announced to me and the rest of the class "Michael, if you or anyone else here today cannot do a pull-up, you can just hang there." How embarrassing! I couldn't wait for my time to be up so I could get down.

As I watched the rest of the kids go one by one up to the bar and do the pull-ups, trying to figure out what was the matter with me. I told myself, "Some people can do things that I can't do. Some people are better than me." There was another peak emotional experience backed up with repetition that added another wall to my box.

What is crazy is from that day on I never thought I could do a pull-up. Whenever it'd be time to do pull-ups in PE or in the gym I'd just say "Oh I can't do pull-ups," and left it at that, until finally one day in my mid-30s I was training for a Spartan race and I had to learn how so I could complete the obstacles. I bought a pull-up bar for my home and practiced a ton so I could get good at it and it was then that I realized that all I had to do was learn how to do it. All this time I thought I could not do something, until one day I realized I simply hadn't learned how to do it yet.

So many limitations are caused in life by split second events, a few words and emotions that shape so much of your life.

But before I realized this, I went through a lot of my life in this box that said "That's for them, not for me." That was my invisible wall. How would I ever go for a new challenge if I thought other people could do things that I couldn't do? Why would I try to achieve something when I knew that I had a history of not being able to figure things out and embarrassing myself in public instead?

I am willing to bet that you've had people with some influence in your life, like my gym teacher, who can say the smallest little comment that rocks your world and changes you forever. My gym teacher was a good guy, meant me no harm, but in that moment he reinforced my inadequate feeling and turned it into a wall I didn't try to push past for twenty-five years.

There are all kinds of boxes that get built for kids by well-meaning adults, and I bet you're walking around with some of them still today. Maybe someone tells you something that sticks with you and immobilizes you. Maybe you look around and see people doing things you don't do or having things you don't have and it creates a box that says you're not as good as the next person.

I took all the input, the General Lee, the pull-ups, the hockey, and the good things, too—and created a box for myself without even knowing it, which in turn decided who I was, shaped my identity and created My Average.

My Average sat inside My Box. My Average was who I was.

THE WALLS GO UP

So let's play this out in your adult life.

You become an adult, have a career, maybe a family, material possessions...you're moving forward achieving goals, maintaining an average and even increasing Your

Average in some areas. That's called maturity and growth. Yet along with those steps forward, you're building the walls of Your Average and making a nice box out of it.

What we're going to do now is understand your box in full detail so you can get a handle on it...and I like to describe this using this box metaphor because it's a simple concept to understand, I'm sure you've already gotten it by now.

Your experiences send messages to your brain that create walls you can't push past and ultimately creates a box that you live in that limits you.

Let's talk about these walls.

That it is Your Average and once you create it, you own it.

WALL #1—YOUR SUPPORT WALL

The wall behind you is the back wall of your box, it supports you and represents what you've surpassed and don't ever want to revisit.

Because you have things in your past that you refuse to accept as Your Average. The wall behind you represents the wall you've pushed through in the past, and everything behind it you want no part of. It's below your current average.

I see this all the time in business where people, in a good way, build their business up to a certain level they accept. They'll excel to a point where they look back and say, "I'll never go back to generating only $X revenue ever again." Or a common one "I will never make under six figures ever again." Or "I'll never work eighty hours a week again." Or whatever it is that they've moved past.

> I've had a caterer tell me, "I'll never go without a sous chef again."
>
> I've had a dentist tell me, "I'll never wash my own linens again."
>
> I've had an internet marketer tell me, "I'll never do a launch that generates under 500K again."
>
> The retail owner says they'll never clean their own store again.
>
> The realtor says they'll never do another open house and miss tneir kid's soccer game.
>
> The pro athlete says, "I'll never accept a contract under 2 million again."

And they mean it—they never go back.

Or in your personal life, the wall behind you might be about settling for the wrong kind of people in the past and refusing to ever do that again. You, by this point, have had enough personal experiences to know what you will and will not accept in your romantic relationships and friendships.

> "I will never be with a person that's high-maintenance again."

> "I'll never settle for someone who doesn't care about my goals."

> "I'll never be with someone who holds me back."

> "I'll never be with someone who is negative and complains about everything."

> "I'll never be with someone who doesn't take care of themselves."

> "I'll never be with someone that has bad habits and won't change them."

> "I'll never be with someone that argues about everything."

Bottom line I'll never settle in a relationship again, and never be with someone that doesn't respect and honor me and my dreams.

This is such a good thing, this wall, because you set your standard of what you must have to be happy and behaviors you will not ever repeat.

When you say, "I don't want to feel that way again," your brain hears you very clearly. It says, "OK, we can't let that happen. We're going to build limitations so you never have to feel that again."

That's the wall behind you.

And once you've decided what you don't want, your mind instantly asks, "Well, if I don't want that, and I won't go there, what do I want?" And so it looks ahead to see what's next, and that's when it runs into the wall in front of you.

WALL #2—YOUR DREAM WALL

The wall in front of you represents every dream, target or goal you have. We've already talked a lot about this wall, and I think you already get it. It was created over time based on experiences that told you what your limits are and set Your Average. It's the wall that keeps you from reaching your dreams.

Yet to be sure to lock it in, let's walk you through how it plays out in your life.

I'm going to share a story with you about a client I've known for over twelve years who had a really great practice, yet it required him to be on-site, adjusting people, day in and day out. Of course he loved his work, loved helping people feel better and be healthier, yet he also wanted to be able to be with his kids and wife more, enjoy life more, be involved in programs where he could mentor people and of course make more money. But every time he went to expand, something went wrong:

- He hired another doctor to come in and work under him, who ended up embezzling money.
- He remodeled his practice and had to pay a fine to a shady landlord looking for a quick buck.
- He hired a practitioner to offer specialized services who then left and solicited his patients.
- He lost thousands to a social media company who made a lot of empty promises.
- He'd hire and train a new receptionist who would flake out.
- He rented space to practitioners offering specialized services who stood around waiting for him to send referrals.

Yet when the opportunity came for him to make the next big push to grow...it meant hiring more staff, bringing on progressive and natural options for his patients, adding in specialized practitioners, buying more equipment and giving up the security of his business as he knows it.

He had a really thick wall in front of him that said, "When you try to grow, something bad happens that costs a lot of time, energy and money."

Now the good news is he'd been to every single one of our events and had highly effective internal communication, so he was able to easily control his emotional and mental state. He saw the wall, took it for what it was, knocked it down and on he went to expand, grow and is thriving as I write this.

But what if he didn't? So what if he felt the invisible wall and kept his average as it was. Doing OK, but Average.

Because most people don't.

While this is all metaphoric, the wall is more real than you can imagine. The wall in front of you represents what you want, what you're aiming at: your target or goals.

"I want to be happy. I want to be a millionaire, I want a Ferrari, I want a beach house, I want a great sex life, I want the perfect relationship. I want it all."

But even wanting it, most people approach the wall and give it a little nudge, see that's rock solid and chicken out.

The wall that has gathered all sorts of references to tell you Your Average.

If you can just get through to the other side, you'll finally get what you want.

WALL #3—YOUR IDENTITY WALL

The 3rd wall dictates who you are, how you show up and what people think of you. Your Identity Wall is the wall on the right because Your Identity will often drive your need to be right in your interactions with people. This part of your identity keeps you Average.

You may have inherited it from your family or culture, or it may have been created through the events in your life—however it became, your identity is the sum total of your individuality, personality, beliefs and self-image.

This is why when you meet someone new to you, you may find yourself weaving into the conversation some little tidbit or fact about you that you want them to know so they will be impressed by you.

It's your Identity talking, and it wants to make sure your identity is clear to this new person. It wants to make sure they see you in the way you want them to, in all your fine glory.

Here you are with the goals you've achieved and the wall behind you that allows you to say, "I'm better than that." You also have huge goals and dreams and plans for your future. They are ever present in the back of your mind as you go about your day, and you aim to do things that are in line with your goals. You push as much as you dare against the wall in front of you.

You work, you do your thing, you live your life and every night you take a shower, brush your teeth, get in bed, set your alarm, put your phone on your nightstand and right next to it, you put your script of who you were today. It's the script you unknowingly keep close at hand because your brain needs it to make sure your life runs on autopilot, to make sure your life is easy.

When you wake up in the morning, either excited or tired, you know in your heart you can be anything you want in the world. You ask yourself, "What's going to happen today? Who am I going to be today?"

Before you can answer, your mind brings your awareness to the easiest and best option that's right there beside you, your script on the nightstand that tells you how you are going to live today, which is the same way you lived yesterday and determines your tomorrow.

And then you do it all over again, every day of the week,

wanting the life you truly desire, but being Your Average you truly are.

Your identity carries the strongest psychological pull to maintain Your Average. You live it, people see it…and that's it.

WALL #4—YOUR RELATIONSHIP WALL

People. People are your 4th wall, the left side of your box, and are there to do one very specific thing: remind you of who you are. They cheer you on, excited for you to be who you are and as you grow out of your box, they will grow with you and be left in your life—or they won't and they'll be left behind.

This 4th wall solidifies your box and is potentially the hardest wall to tear down.

Take a look around at the people in your life. Some are right beside you as you go for your goals, and want you to Raise Your Average and get out of your box. They believe in you and support you.

There are also the people that are there because Your Average keeps them there. These people are there to keep you safe, to make sure your life works the way you designed it. At the same time they are keeping you inside your box. They are happy to support you as you continue being the person you are. Anything else makes them uncomfortable—whether they say it out loud or not.

Your relationships will remind you what's OK to make economically, they challenge you, drive you nuts, waste your time, push you to live up to your potential, send you in strange directions, and/or encourage you to realize that it's OK to be who you are. All of it, depending on who they are and depending on Their Average.

Even with people who want you to get out of your box, the relationship you have with them is built in a way that needs you to be who you are so that they feel good about themselves.

You must decide who you want by your side.

I'll say this once, the people in your life will grow with you, keep you where you are or hold you back.

You must decide before you attempt to get out of your box to surround yourself with people that want you to get out.

Because if you're attempting to take with you someone who's reinforcing the 4th wall you won't get out.

Get that?

So what if the people in your life have an average they aren't interested in improving?

You're going to have to figure this part out.

I'll say that again so you really hear me...*you're going to have to figure this part out.*

If you're married to that person, you're going to have to improve your communication so you can influence them to grow with you and get them to join you in creating a new average.

If you're in business with someone that doesn't want your business to grow in the same way you do, you're going to have to improve your communication so you can get on the same page or find a way to work together.

If your friends are the jealous type, you're probably going to have to find new friends.

If your friends have pitiful goals, you're going to have to inspire them to want more, or soon you'll have nothing to talk about.

If your family is toxic, you're going to have to improve

your communication so you can improve those tense conversations around the Thanksgiving table.

If you want out of the box, you'll have to ask yourself the difficult question: "Are these the people I need in my life to pull it off?" Because if they're not, they will contribute to Your Average that controls you.

If your relationship wall is going to be hard to tear down, I encourage you to get started on that right away because you're going to require some of the most powerful communication skills you can gain to make it happen. I know this because this is what I spend my days doing...teaching communication skills. Any challenge you have with people can be resolved through powerful communication.

With the right people, you can easily get to your desired Average.

So those are your walls, that is your box. Since the last thing you're asking yourself is, "How do I become more of who I am?" let's get the answer to "How do I get out of the box or through the wall to get what I want?"

OUT OF THE BOX

By now you're probably questioning everything about your life.

Hopefully so.

Hopefully you're already planning how you're going to get out of your box and evaluating your friends, your identity, your walls.

Good news: you can become a quick-change artist.

Change *can* happen quickly. So while you may be frustrated at where you are, there's no need to feel overwhelmed by where you want to go.

You see, contrary to popular belief, change is not always hard when done right. Actually it can happen rather quickly. Real lasting change, which is what most people seek when they walk in my office, can happen in an instant or it can happen over time based on repetition.

All it takes for an instant change is a peak emotional experience.

The intensity of the experience determines how quickly the change occurs. (You'll learn more about this later.) We've all experienced quick change. You reach for a cookie, burn your hand on the stove, and you know not to touch a hot stove ever again. Instant change.

Quick change can be positive as well. It happened to my

younger daughter last year when she won the Citizenship Award at her school. She went from being a kid that was kind and helpful to a kid that won an award. Instant change. The moment she was honored in front of her classmates she knew that being kind wasn't just our family values, it was something that the world recognizes and must be part of her life permanently.

You can think back right now and recall a thousand times you've heard a tragic story followed by "they were never the same again."

I tell you that so you fully understand that no matter the situation, good or bad, instant change can happen when something out of the norm occurs, which is really great news for you.

When you experience instant change, you have a New Average, and you're immediately out of the box!

More good news: slow and steady wins the race.

Now if there's not a peak emotional experience to bring about instant change, you can always rely on repetition to make sure the change happens.

We all have heard it takes twenty-one days to create a habit. For years we believed that a reward was necessary to help make a habit stick...the proverbial carrot. Yet there's new and even better research out today that says if you repeat a behavior, even if it's not enjoyable to you and there's no reward, the action taken will stick just as easily and become Your New Average. How about that for incentive!

Theoretically that means you can go to the gym, and hate going, repeatedly and consistently, it will turn into an automatic behavior that you enjoy. You won't have to force yourself to go, you will automatically go!

Let's think of some other examples of repetition that create change:

Imagine if you've been smoking for years and Your Average is a smoker. But then one day you decide to be a nonsmoker, so you don't smoke the next day, or the next, or the next...until the repetition of not smoking created a New Average for you. After enough repetition, there's nothing that could make you want to smoke.

How about people that make prospecting calls for work? Nobody picks up the phone on the first call and knows exactly what to say, how to say it and *comfortably* gets the prospect to the next step in the sales pipeline. It takes making thousands of calls before a person gets really good on the phone.

So you want out of your box, you repeat a behavior that will raise Your Average, and then Your New Average will get you out of your box.

Either way, in order to get out of the box, Your Average must increase.

BUT WHAT ABOUT ME, SINCE I'M DIFFERENT?

You may be thinking, "I'm a highly motivated, driven person. Why don't I just do the Nike thing, just do it, and push through to the other side of the wall?"

A lot of people do this. They go to a personal development seminar, they listen to motivational podcasts, or they watch YouTube videos about how to hustle, and they get fired up. They lower their shoulders and run as hard as they can, and they slam into the wall of what they want. They push, and they push, and they push...but they're still in the box.

The problem—other than a sore shoulder—is that they're trying to push through the wall, instead of recognizing that Their Average isn't high enough and they are stuck.

The only way you'll ever get out of the box is to grow big enough to step out of it.

IN SEARCH OF A SOLUTION

I see you nodding again. You're probably thinking, "OK, Michael. I get it. I need adversity, I need challenges, I'll push myself to do things I don't normally do."

Let's recap:

- You accept that you have a box that controls your Average, and you don't like it.
- You change your perceptions, either in an instant or over time.
- You take actions that will raise Your Average.
- You get out of the box into a new one.
- Good things come your way.

This is a foolproof plan, and the only thing that will slow you down is Your Current Average.

That's OK, you'll find your way, I know you will. Because Average Sucks and you want no part of that.

USING ADVERSITY TO YOUR ADVANTAGE

It's time to seek out adversity.

We already realized you need it to get out of your box.

Now you must realize that the adversity you need, the

"rebirth" of it in your life, will come in the form of your four walls.

You've got to get really good at seeing what it is for what it is.

Let's say you step on the scale and see that you've gained five or ten pounds. Instantly you flinch, you may even get depressed. Or you look at your bank statement and you have less than you thought and have to pull back on your spending. You get pissed. You see your neighbors doing better than you, and you get jealous. You think, "Why are things so easy for them?"

What if I told you that all of this was simply misfired emotions and your inability to use adversity to your advantage? Misreading these messages causes the majority of the problems in your life. Misreading these messages causes you to accept Your Average and strengthens the walls of your box.

When you see this clearly, you realize that gaining ten pounds is your body's way of telling you that it's time to get to the gym. You have a built-in trainer telling you to do something different. Feeling uncomfortable when you see your negative bank balance is what motivates you to do better in your business.

What if adversity is just your wall talking, coaching you to the next level, doing its best to inspire you, asking you if you really want to become who you say you want to be.

When you feel a little pang of jealousy over your neighbor's new car, it's your brain saying, "Learn from them how to do it. Have the courage to go up and ask how they're growing their business so rapidly."

When your coworker takes a fun vacation with their teenager and you can't get your teenager to do much more than mumble, it's your signal to work on your communication skills so you can connect with them.

Most people just experience the emotions and miss that they're there for a reason. When you run into adversity, it's telling you to pay attention, that there's something to learn.

Because our current society encourages us to seek comfort and avoid adversity, we are not that familiar with adversity, and it doesn't really exist in the world as often anymore, we can hide from it. We don't need to deal with it. We accept our reality. You accept your identity. You accept Your Average as being overweight, underpaid, and not doing well as other people.

Do not accept Your Average.

ADVERSITY AWAITS

My license plate reads "Average Sucks" for a reason. It's a constant reminder that Your Average will never make you happy. Whatever you do on a regular basis is great, but it's not going to lead you where your heart wants you to go.

And the solution isn't about what you know. I couldn't care less about what you know; I care about what you're capable of doing and what you actually do on a regular basis. If you have the greatest workout routine in the world but you can't get yourself to do it, that routine doesn't matter. It's about getting yourself to do these things that truly make a difference.

Motivation isn't going to do anything either, perspective will. There are two ways to change your life: change your actions, or change your perspective. If you change your actions, you might go to the gym a few more times. Yet if you change your perception to see yourself as a person who works out, and you get the world to see you that way, then that becomes what you do.

Do you see how this goes hand in hand with the change we talked about earlier?

Instant change happens with an immediate change in perspective, which results in a change in your actions.

Change over time happens with repetition, and that repetition will change your perspective which will change Your Average which will change who you are.

So how do you get started?

So you live inside a box. It doesn't matter what you know or what you've done before. It doesn't matter what you're capable of if you're not doing anything.

Get out-of-the-box thinking means learning to play differently than you currently play.

Let's start moving into next-level thinking. The first step is to understand something very basic: today is a starting line. It is the beginning of something big. And every day is a new starting line. It's the beginning of what we're doing.

Again, it's not about having a plan; it's about doing something.

Years ago, my buddy Jordan asked me to be on his conference call. "At the end, I'd like you to offer something to the group, some sort of call to action something they can use to follow up with you."

In that moment I was uncomfortable...I didn't have anything. My Average showed up and in an instant I was a guy with nothing to show.

So I took the adversity and moved fast, making up a course on the spot.

"I don't really have a name," I told him, "so I'll call it Call2Action. How does that sound?"

There were 300 people on that conference call, and 150 of them invested in the Call2Action course that I offered. Here's the problem: I didn't have a course to deliver to them.

Business 101 says to just get started, so that's what I did: I got started. I used adversity to my advantage and created a New Average for myself.

I built a program that showed people how to communicate with themselves, got them moving and radically changed their perceptions about who they were and what their life could be. Since then Call2Action has been shared with countless people all over the world and changed the lives and families of thousands of people.

It didn't start with a grandiose plan. I didn't build this big sales funnel and spend hours in my basement building a prototype. I had a challenge...I was coaching people one-on-one and there are only so many hours in the day. I was offered an opportunity to work with a large group of people and I needed to move fast, so I did. There's no way to measure the ripple effect of that decision, yet it's a decision that allowed me, in my way, to impact the world for the better.

What will you do? What could you do today that would position you to get out of your box?

I'll tell you what I would do if I were you, reading this book, thinking about Average.

I'll tell you what I would tell my clients if they were sitting across from me.

I'd tell them to write down three things:

1. What is your next outcome, your next goal you want to accomplish?
2. What is the biggest challenge you'll have to overcome to get out of your box which is keeping you from achieving that outcome?
3. What will you do to raise Your Average so you are able to get out of your box?

Let me give you an example of a client so you can get an idea of how this would go.

Here's Tom Adams, a successful businessman who had put in hours, days, months and years to get where he was in his career. A lot of years, over forty of them in fact. He was established, successful and happy...and also ready to slow down a little bit. His next big outcome was to get his business on autopilot so he could spend more time away from the office doing things he enjoyed.

His biggest challenge was his business partner. They didn't see eye to eye on many things and because of their differences, the business didn't run as well as it could. And it certainly wasn't ready to run on autopilot while the partner was still in the picture. It was obvious to Tom that if he wanted to get his business positioned for him to relax, he'd have to either influence his partner to perform better or ditch him. There's his wall.

The 4th wall of relationships which caused feelings of guilt, obligation, frustration, expectation...all of them preventing him from pushing past the wall so he could enjoy his life. If you want to take an aerial picture of this situation, Tom was living his life for his partner, and it wasn't even his wife!

So we worked on this together, and Tom learned that his communication with his partner would have to improve dramatically for him to achieve his outcome. He began to work on his own internal communication, managing his emotional state when things didn't go well, which put him in the right position to have effective conversations. He worked on his external communication, learning how to connect with his partner to have productive conversations and move forward, rather than coming to a standstill.

Over time, he was able to peacefully come to an agreement with his partner that it was time for him to move on. Now Tom is free to make the choices he wants to make in his own company, get his business on autopilot in a way he's comfortable with, and enjoy the life he's worked all these years to create.

Sounds so easy, right? It is that easy, as long as you are committed to achieving the skills you need. That's what I mean when I say you must get around Above Average information. This is a perfect example of a person that sought to understand human behavior and communication, making him able to knock down the wall and get out of his box.

Look, you're going to have a box and you're going to have an average. There's nothing wrong with that! I encourage you to be certain that you are *selecting* Your Average, and *selecting* the box you're currently in, knowing there will be another when you're ready to grow bigger.

CHAPTER 3

ACCEPT YOUR AVERAGE

Early on in my business, I came into an extra $30,000. To me, that felt like $10 million. What do you do if you suddenly find yourself with an extra $10 million? Or even $30,000?

I had no idea what to do with it, so I called the financial planner my parents recommended and said, "I have some money, and I'd like to turn it into more money."

"OK," he said. "Sounds great. What would you like to do with the money?"

"I don't know. I'd like to give it to you so you can make more money with it."

"I understand," he replied, "but are you looking to buy a house? Pay back debt? Are you saving for your future, for retirement?"

I still didn't know. "I have thirty grand. I'd like it to be more, and you can put me in as aggressive an account as you have."

He had to really spell it out for me. "Without understanding your plan, there's no way I'm going to be able to help you pull off what you're looking for. It would be an abuse of my fiduciary responsibilities if I don't understand where you currently are and where you want to go."

Sound familiar?

I had to know where I was and where I wanted to go. I had one of the answers—I wanted to go wherever I could make more money—but where was I starting from?

WHERE YOU ARE

At that time, I didn't even realize I had an average. I certainly hadn't accepted it. But you can get there faster than I did. You just have to Accept Your Average.

Accepting Your Average means understanding what you're truly dealing with and what you're up against. Like the financial planner, I can't show you how to get what you want until you first know where you are.

Most people aren't willing to take that look. They hide their heads in the sand and let what they really want pass them by.

Lucky for you, you're not like most people.

There's no way to calculate an actual number on Your Average. Yet what we can do is come up with an understanding of all the important pieces in your life.

Every single client I've ever had, and I believe this is true for every person on the planet, has the same three categories of life they look to improve.

- Physical Health
- Relationship Health
- Financial Health

So if we investigate how well you're doing in each of these areas, we can assess where you are and identify what you must work on first to raise Your Average.

Since every person is different, there's no standard mean for each of these categories.

To one person, physical health may mean simply being at an ideal weight, having plenty of energy and looking nice in their clothes. To another, physical health may mean you're as ripped as Shaun T (who's Beachbody Insanity and T25 DVDs are permanent fixtures in our house) and it makes you extremely happy to spend time physically challenging yourself at a high level.

Let's say you're starting out in your career and enjoying your life, have no desire to get married anytime soon; relationship health to you means having great friends you enjoy spending time with in your free time. But to another, it may mean trying to bring back the passion in a lackluster marriage where it seems like you're living with a roommate instead of the love of your life.

Financial health may mean you have no debt, ten million in savings and consistently adding to it, whereas another person may have a financial goal of paying off their house and cars, paying for college for their two kids and funding their 401(k) so they can live off of it after they retire.

You get the point, everyone is different so there's no way to create a formula or calculation, yet you can come up with a general idea of where you are.

ASSESSING YOUR AVERAGE

I've included a simple assessment to help you understand Your Average. It's not a formal evaluation and it's not scientific, it's merely here as a simple tool to help you get what you want.

YOUR AVERAGE ASSESSMENT

Physical Health

On a scale of 0-10, what score would you give your Physical Health?

0 1 2 3 4 5 6 7 8 9 10

Factors to consider:

- Eating Habits
- Exercise
- Medications
- Supplements
- Sleep
- Stress
- Living Environment

Relationship Health

On a scale of 0-10, what score would you give your Relationship Health?

0 1 2 3 4 5 6 7 8 9 10

Factors to consider:

- Communication
- Open Mindedness
- Trust
- Respect
- Companionship
- Arguing Style
- Honesty
- Passion

Financial Health

On a scale of 0-10, what score would you give your Financial Health?

0 1 2 3 4 5 6 7 8 9 10

Factors to consider:

- Spending Habits
- Savings
- Income
- Income Potential
- Insurance Policies
- Credit Score
- Assets
- Retirement Planning
- Estate Planning

There's no correct or exact way to complete this assessment, yet I would encourage you to honestly rate yourself in each area with these questions in mind:

1. Am I considering all the factors when I assess myself?
2. Am I considering my full potential, or where I'm at now?
3. Am I considering a general consensus, what the world at large would agree with?

Answering this honestly will give you Your Average.

Accepting Your Average will give you your starting point.

Now, take all three categories and do your best to average them together to give you your total score. And here's where the rubber meets the road. Because how many people do you know that are wildly successful are overweight? How many people do you know that have a rock hard body have no money in the bank?

Many people hide their Below Average score in one category with their super high average score in another, and that's not a great way to live. Wouldn't that be easy? I don't want anyone walking around with all kinds of accolades and awards and money in the bank but then going home every night to a house filled with tension. That Average Sucks.

Averaging everything together will give you a true, accurate score and lead you to having the life of your dreams.

Now, write down Your Average, sign and date it.

My Average ______________________________

Signature ______________________________

Today's Date ______________________________

AVERAGE: ACCEPTED

When you accept Your Average, you understand where you really are so you can then do something about it.

You'll be dealing with Your Average for the rest of your life. It's never going to go away. It's your shadow; you can't chase it or run away from it.

At so many stages of my life, I got stuck at new averages, inside a new box. You will, over the time in your life, raise Your Average and get a new box, only to find that after some time it doesn't serve you anymore. That's OK, you'll continue the process and continue to grow. That's the beauty of life.

The other day I did a training for a group of real estate

investors and I asked them what their Average was when it came to their ability to communicate and influence others. When they shared their self score, most were high numbers, 8s and 9s. Then I asked them to score themselves based on their potential, not just where they currently were, but where they could be if they used their intelligence, resources, etc.

The room went silent.

They realized in that moment that no matter what score you give yourself, there is always room to grow. For the rest of the training I noticed how much more engaged they were; they sat taller in their chairs, went to the restroom less and asked a ton of questions. They wanted to be more effective.

Now, if you're ready to Raise Your Average, the next chapter is going to show you exactly what I did for myself and hundreds of thousands of people all over the world to raise our average and become who we wanted to be.

If you're ready, scream those immortal words: "Average Sucks!"

It's time to change Your Average.

CHAPTER 4

ADMIT WHAT YOU WANT

In my mind, Michael Werner could do anything.

We all know people like this: confident, powerful in his communication, capable of handling any situation. If you put this guy in charge of running your business, you *know* he would do a great job.

Michael Werner was the name on my fake ID.

Until I turned twenty-one, Michael Werner was, well, *me*. But not just any me—the best version of me. The *me* I wanted to be.

I'd flash that plastic card with Michael Werner's name

and my picture to the bouncer and walk into the club with all the confidence (and arrogance) in the world. I walked tall, charismatic, talked easily to anyone and rolled with whatever came my way. Michael Werner knew how to have fun. He was magnetic, never got rattled and the life of the party.

What started out as a Fake ID became my new Fake Identity...Mr. Party Guy and I loved every minute of it. I went out all the time; drinking, laughing, having fun, organizing and orchestrating one social scene after the other.

And guess what, it was never me. I was acting the entire time making sure people liked me, respected me, wanted to be around me, all of that.

Sure I was a fun guy and liked being around people, but to be that magnanimous, no that wasn't me. From the outside it looked like I had a pretty high Average, but it wasn't real and on the inside guess what I felt...Average.

It wasn't until years later, long after I got busted for my fake ID and had to pay the price, that I realized why it's far easier to pretend to be someone else than it is to be all of yourself.

KNOW WHO YOU ARE

Michael Werner was at first just a fake ID I needed to get into bars, but then became a part I played to make myself feel better until I learned to like myself, and that's what most people are doing: playing a part. They act a part when they need to show up well in situations, but they play smaller than they're capable of, instead of being all of themselves.

Years ago I ran a public speaking program where I taught individuals how to design and deliver a captivating presentation. Almost every person that attended—doctors, lawyers, sales professionals, business owners, people from all different industries—had an average presentation they'd been doing, often for decades, that got them average results.

By the time the program was over they owned presentation skills that were radically different from anything they'd done before. I had shy people and dynamic people and it didn't matter—by the time they went home they were comfortable speaking, highly effective, engaging and completely outside their current box.

During the first half of the class, we'd work on content, second half we'd work on delivery. I noticed in the beginning that most everyone was really great at crafting their new messages. They could gather their material and write out a presentation script that was sure to impress the audience and get them to take action.

They were ready to go with everything they needed to present, except one thing...they were uncomfortable. It wasn't necessarily the fear of public speaking, though that is a fear for many people; they were uncomfortable with themselves. They held back talking about who they were and why they were up there selling their product or presenting this material.

Most of the time people will stand up and deliver content and remove themselves from the message, which is boring. I'd helped them craft a presentation weaving stories throughout the content, incorporating their identity into the conversation to bring depth and credibility. That's the part where they locked up. They could talk about details but not about themselves.

During one event, I teamed up two guys to work on their presentations together. They gave each other feedback on their content and delivery. One was a British gentleman named Nigel and the other Brad, a super smart real estate guy from California with a lot of experience, and apparent confidence. When it was time to present to the entire group, Brad got up to speak first, and even though he'd been in the business for twenty years and practiced his presentation, he bombed.

He lacked enthusiasm, rambled and he certainly didn't engage the audience. This confident, smart guy who should have nailed it, bombed.

After he sat down, I asked Nigel to stand up. He was a coach, someone who motivated people and helped them make their lives better. He'd never done any real estate investing before, but when I asked him to give Brad's presentation the best he could—he killed it. He gave a stellar presentation on Brad's topic. Nigel convinced the entire room of the benefits of being a real estate investor, how to get started, and how much money we could make from investing. He spoke with passion and excitement and enthusiasm—because he was *acting like Brad*.

Nigel, in an instant, took Brad's content and delivered it in the way he knew Brad would want to deliver it. It was incredible.

So Brad's sitting there watching Nigel deliver his presentation and all the light bulbs went on. He had to own *who he was* and deliver his presentation as the best version of himself. To prove the point and to show everyone how powerful they can be, I then asked Brad to stand up and give Nigel's presentation, which he did, perfectly—complete with a British accent!

Why is it so much easier to pretend to be someone else

than to be fully who you are? Because we are innately uncomfortable with our Average! If you want to get out of your box and generate a New Average for your life, you must stop being *part* of you and start owning and being *all* of you.

ADMIT WHAT YOU WANT

One of the first things you must do to be all of you is to admit and own what you truly want. It's one of the biggest battles we have in life; admitting what we want and then actually going out and getting it. You get why, right? Every time you admit what you really want, your Dream Wall starts yelling at you, reminding you of Your Average.

To get around that, every time you admit what you want. it's equally as important to admit where you're really starting from.

And yes, admitting where you're starting from, your Current Average, will only highlight the disparity between where you are now and where you want to go, which is no fun.

Yet, admitting where you are immediately forces you to acknowledge that you're not where you want to be. You've worked so hard to be who you are, getting up every day and working (sometimes grinding) just to get here.

Average. It's painful to admit that where you are is not where you want to be.

You're OK, you're in the right place. Average Sucks, you don't like it and above all—you now know the feeling you're having is the Adversity you need to grow. You're going to use this to your advantage.

Yes, human beings tend to avoid pain. *But not you because you're ready to get out of the box*. Adversity is the spark that helps you get where you want to go.

Take sports for an example. If offense played just as well as defense—nobody would score. How boring would that be? There'd be no contest.

My wife and I typically go to every activity our girls are involved in. This is part of our Average. Would they be OK if we missed something, yes. Do we want to? No. We've created a flexible life that allows us to be at almost every activity because we want to support our girls in this way. One of the side benefits of being there to watch our oldest cheer on the sidelines is getting to watch a lot of basketball, football and soccer games. And it's fun, especially when the game is suspenseful. One night we're watching this basketball game that went into quadruple overtime. You get what happened, back and forth—they score, we score, tie, they score, we score, tie. In the 4th overtime our team scored and won.

Did they beat the other team? Yes.

They also beat their own average. Check this out:

> In the game, they played their Average.
>
> In first overtime, they played their Average.
>
> In second overtime, they played their Average.
>
> In third overtime, they played their Average.
>
> In 4th overtime, they got out of the box.

Going into quadruple overtime was an adversity that taught those boys a great lesson. The biggest reason we find it challenging to improve our Average is because we look at the challenge as a negative instead of recognizing it for what it is: a starting point. It's not a negative, it's where it all begins.

Think about how much fun that 4th overtime game was. What if you looked at your Adversity, your Dream Wall, as a game instead of agonizing over it, struggling with it, fighting it. Remember I said you can't push through the wall. You must grow bigger than the box.

Growing up, we had a wall in our house where my dad would mark a line at the top of my head to track how tall I was growing. My sister had her lines, too. It was so fun watching the lines go up and up! What if you thought about your growth that way, and embraced the adversity as a means to the end?

All I'm saying is look at the bright side! Besides, who wants to be around a complainer? You pick:

> Person 1: "Ugh, I have to go to the gym, I get so sweaty, I am so tired, I hate the treadmill, the weights hurt my shoulder, the instructor goes too fast and I can't keep up." Blah, blah, blah, bleh.
>
> Person 2: "I didn't feel like it yet I pushed myself and went to the gym and worked out. The gym was super busy, so I didn't get much time on my favorite machine but I tried a new one and it was awesome. I'm so proud of myself!"

I can promise you, I'd tune out the first person and ask the second person to call me when they want to go hike Camelback mountain.

I can also promise you that the second person will be out of their box much sooner.

You must lean into the concept of admitting that where

you are now is not where you want to be. If you act like everything's OK, your brain is never going to start looking for new solutions. This isn't a negative; if you're not where you want to be, you're in a phenomenal place. You have room to grow, and admitting that is just the spark you've been looking for.

It's time to get what you want.

ACCELERATE YOUR AVERAGE

Throughout this book I'm going to share with you little strategies you will use to make it easy to apply what you learn. At my events I don't just hand out concepts and let everyone go figure it out, we integrate with tools to make things happen.

The Average Accelerator is one of those strategies.

It's a little game to truly accelerate how fast you Raise Your Average. Some people would call it a hack, but it's really a change of perception. Remember back in chapter 1 when I said you must change your perception, which changes your actions, which changes your results? This is a tool to help you do that.

The Average Accelerator is a game of Target Practice. To play the game, I want you to imagine that you have a target game board out in front of you, and inside the bullseye are your *non-negotiables.*

What does that mean?

Anything negotiable is up for discussion, there's flexibility, we can talk about it.

Non-negotiables shut any other ideas down. It's the "No Soliciting" sign outside a building, it's the contract you signed, the hand you shook and it means that whatever has already been decided is the way it is.

As you look at the target in front of you, imagine if you put every single non-negotiable in your life in the bullseye. Right in the middle.

These non-negotiables are the things you know that you must do: go to work, make money, exercise, stick to your commitments. If you're married, hopefully you're committed to coming home each night—that usually keeps you married. Your non-negotiables might include picking up your kids from school, taking your vitamins, or paying your rent or mortgage on time. We all have a lot of non-negotiables in our lives, and they are specific to you and your life. Yours are different than mine, and mine are different than my neighbor, and so on.

Now without knowing what I mean in advance, if I asked you to make a list of your non-negotiables, you might write down things that you know you want to accomplish; "Making a million dollars" or "Going to the gym every day."

But is it? Have you done it before? For most people, the answer is no.

You may say that having a great body is a non-negotiable, but if you don't currently have one then it is completely negotiable.

Real, legitimate non-negotiables are things that you are going to do *no matter what*. You don't even have to think about them; they're going to happen. These non-negotiables are Your Average, and they are where you spend the majority of the time, energy and money in your life.

Surrounding that small bullseye of non-negotiables are the additional, bigger rings on your game board, but the truth is you pretty much ignore those because you're preoccupied with your bullseye. You keep shooting at the important things in the bullseye because, of course, who wouldn't want all those points, right?

That's such a bad play. Get this, while you're so busy

shooting at the things that are non-negotiable, you're missing out on the bigger game.

Every now and then we go to the bowling alley and after we bowl a game and my younger daughter's attention span has given out, we go over to the arcade and play a little Speed Racing, Skee Ball and maybe even Dance Dance Revolution. Every time one of us hits that 100 point cup in the corner there's a ton of celebrating because the tickets are about to come flying out of the machine and there's going to be a lot of fun at the prize counter. That's an arcade high I'm talking about but what about your life? That 100 point cup represents all the things you want. Those are the things that are going to raise Your Average. Those are the things that will get you out of the box.

To get the wants you want, and eventually your dreams, the trick is to make the bullseye bigger. Are you getting this? When you change your perception and expand the bullseye and fill it with negotiables (converting them to non-negotiables) all of a sudden you must take the actions that will ensure you complete those items. You must, because they're non-negotiables.

Now yes, it's easier said than done for some. Maybe you'll expand your bullseye a lot, maybe just a little. Either way gets your wants as musts and on the way to your dreams.

I'm not asking you to make a huge circle, I'm asking you to expand, grow bigger, raise Your Average.

And yes, it will work. Doing this will Accelerate your actions and Accelerate Your Average.

For years, I've taught people that if you want something, you can want it for the rest of your life. But if you work on what you want—your business, your communication, your confidence—Your Average goes up. Going to Toastmasters to become a better speaker, going to the gym, taking martial arts, working on your patience by taking yoga, really working on your relationship—eventually what you want becomes non-negotiable.

When I was twenty-two years old, the thought of me owning a home was completely negotiable. But once I became a husband and a father and we bought a home, signed the paperwork, and got the keys, it became non-negotiable. I didn't just buy a house, I moved owning a home to my bullseye. Get it?

The Average Accelerator is a power play—move more of your wants into your center bullseye, change your perspective of the item to non-negotiable, and you're on your way to getting what you want.

Soon enough you'll be ready to go for your dreams and

expand your bullseye to include those dreams. How high will Your Average be when your Non-Negotiables include your dreams?

WANTS VS. DREAMS

Now let's talk about the specific things you want. I'm not going to ask you to make your dream list, but we do need to make an important distinction between *wants* and *dreams*. People feel frustrated when they don't understand the difference between a want and a dream.

A *want* is having a better body or getting in better shape. A *want* is having more money or a new car. A *want* is improving your relationship or writing a book.

A *dream*, on the other hand, is big. A dream would be Oprah endorsing your book. A *dream* would be going from overweight soccer mom to a fitness model or owning four houses with live-in butlers. A dream would be building your business up, taking it public and retiring early. A dream would be playing in the NHL, just saying.

Yes, you should go for your dreams, yet let's get there progressively so it lasts. In the meantime you must accept that your wants will lead you to those dreams. Work on your wants first.

I can't tell you how many clients I have that are internet marketers in search of a big launch. They want a promo that'll make millions and they're always looking for the next big hit. I always ask them, why not be OK with a few thousand to get started?

What you want is to be great at internet marketing and rake in loads of cash, I get it. Yet to truly get great at it, you'll be wise to consistently raise Your Average over time. People are happy to make a thousand dollars but nobody wants to make ten bucks. This is why people in the internet marketing industry have such highs and lows and go from rolling in the big life and posting all their fancy activities on social media, to dropping off and going dark for big chunks of time. Then they're back again with their next big launch.

I'd much prefer a steady and consistent growth without all that stress. Their Average is to be on a roller coaster. There's no sense in that. This is dream chasing and skipping over the wants. It's not increasing Your Average and getting out of your box.

Here's an example: the very first live event I ever did was tiny. I think we had fifty people in the room, getting everything organized on the fly and definitely freaking out about the expensive hotel minimums. It was a real push to make that event happen and I'll tell you now like I'd have told you then—I was thrilled with those fifty people. Did I want 500? Of course! Would I rather have more people in the room so I could afford the hotel space and make a better profit? Of course! Yet I knew it was a *dream* to fill a huge room, what I *wanted* was to hold a life-changing event where people paid for tickets, came to an event, got the transformation they were looking for, and went home with a higher Average.

What if that wouldn't have been good enough?

What if I was only interested in a huge event with lots of people and a big fancy setup. It would have taken me a few more years of building before I could have that type of an event, and waiting for that would have been ridiculous and shortsighted. My Average would have stayed the same, I wouldn't have created momentum for my business, I wouldn't have met those fifty awesome people and I wouldn't have changed their lives.

Be OK with the want, it'll get you out of the box and onto your dreams.

It's truly a simple mindset shift and it works.

WORK ON WHAT YOU WANT

So let's work on those *wants*. The first question you

must figure out is this—where do you spend your time, thoughts, energy, and money on a regular basis?

Your effort currently goes toward maintaining Your Average, maintaining what you have, instead of getting what you want. But now you're going to spend more time working on what you want and making your non-negotiable bullseye target bigger.

Little by little, your actions will create change and raise Your Average. Remember, the time you spend repeating the actions needed to create change will make them permanent. Likely it will be new and uncomfortable at first, yet along the way you will develop skills and it will become easier to you, second nature.

Years ago I was talking about *wants* vs. *dreams* at an event when a man, Derrick, raised his hand and told me his dream was to be a photographer. At the time, though, he was a busy single dad who worked for a semiconductor company. He didn't have a ton of extra time to work on his photography, and his camera wasn't good enough to take professional pictures. He was stuck. Stuck doing what he always did, stuck being his Average.

As he went through the event he worked on his communication; learning how to manage his mental and emotional state, build his confidence and stay consistently motivated to work on this dream.

After that, Derrick decided to buy a professional camera, a real growth move for his situation. That act of working on his wants moved owning a camera from his wants to his non-negotiables. He started playing around, taking pictures, until someone eventually asked, "Hey, will you shoot my kid's birthday party? I'll give you a hundred bucks."

He committed to doing it and boom, there went his Average. Up! He shot pictures for the party and got paid. This growth move made his bullseye bigger, being a paid photographer was now non-negotiable. Next step, make the dream a non-negotiable, but how could he do that with a full-time job?

Derrick kept doing the part-time gigs for a couple years, making a hundred bucks here and a couple hundred bucks there. He made maybe a few thousand dollars his first year, and used the money to buy some extra equipment and take some classes.

Then, in 2008, the economy tanked. Derrick was laid off from his job at the semiconductor company. But he's a single dad, and he had to make money.

Well, he was a man with a camera and a paid photographer. Now he had to make another shift, change his identity and raise his personal Average. He had to ignore the Dream Wall in front of him that had a lot of negative things to say..."You can't make enough money as a full-time photographer." "There's a lot of competition, you're not as good as some of these other photographers," "Being a photographer isn't a real job." He had to grow bigger than that wall and get out of the box, so he did.

He went from being a part-time photographer to a high-demand, full-time photographer. He soon had a long list of clients asking him to shoot weddings, engagements, parties, graduations, baby pictures, you name it. He even shot one of my events! He kept pushing himself, kept growing until, eventually, his dreams moved into the bullseye. He dreamed of being a photographer, and now he makes a living with his camera. Being a photographer is now a non-negotiable.

As you face the walls of your box, you'll grow and overcome them. You will! Your wants become non-negotiables, and eventually your dreams come closer, too. You will find ways to make the things you *want* part of *who you are*.

KILLING OFF THE OLD YOU

The old you, your Old Average, is great. It got you here.

There's an indisputable value in the box you were in, the Average you had. You can be proud of where you are, yet right now you've decided that OK was OK, but now OK is not OK and you're ready to move on. Grow.

This means you are ready to accept the death of your old identity (which changes your Identity Wall) and accept that your Current Average dominates you.

The second you admit you're not where you want to be, the process starts immediately—so do it now.

After you admit it to yourself, you've got to be real about it with the people around you. I talk a lot about congruency, which means what you say and what you do lines up perfectly. You know what I mean, walk the talk, practice what you preach, follow through on your words.

When I talk about congruency, I can't emphasize enough that if you are incongruent, it decreases your confidence. If you're living a lie, or you're faking it, your unconscious knows it and it doesn't like it. Believe me, you don't want to be sending the wrong messages to your brain, and it's listening all the time.

Here's a simple way of understanding it: How many times do you respond, "I'm great!" when asked how you're doing. I'm not saying to give random people your sob story nor should you dump your latest challenge on the nice parent standing next to you at your kid's practice. Why not take a more honest approach to an innocent question.

The next time someone asks, "How are you?" why not respond with "I'm doing well, right now I'm spending a lot of time working on my networking skills so I can get more clients." Or "I'm doing well, I'm exercising more consistently because I want to have more energy to chase these kids around!" When said casually, it comes across as a natural answer and more importantly, it's the truth.

I already told you when I was taking on the identity of Michael Werner, I was really a fraud. I pretended to be someone I wasn't and it kept me Average. Interestingly enough, the same thing happened recently in my business. We're growing and wonderful things are happening, clients are happy, everyone was healthy, all was good. However, my wife and I weren't sleeping enough.

Why?

Because we were working a ton of hours and that, coupled with our commitment to be involved in our kids' lives and activities, meant that we were up late and up early. Mind you, we enjoy our work, and don't mind what we were doing, yet we were overloaded. We wanted to find additional people to come work on our team, more clients, more connections, we needed help!

Nobody offered, and we didn't ask. From the outside it looked like we were cranking and didn't need help. We weren't pretending, everything *was* good! Our business was booming yet we were doing it all ourselves! Which meant we weren't fully admitting our Average, which was lower than it could be because we weren't asking for help.

And I bet you can relate to that one.

Right away, switch things up and be real with the people around you. The next time someone asks how you're doing, don't answer, "Great, perfect, everything's fine." It's better to say where you are. We live in a world where most people try to be like everybody else and put their best foot forward.

Your life will be so much better, Your Average so much higher, when you are all of who you are, and real about it.

In our case, we joined three high level masterminds and built a new network where we could openly ask for help and receive it and extend help back in the opposite direction wherever we could. It's been beneficial both in business and in Our Average.

It's time to move on. All of this makes the process possible, go quicker and less frustrating. This is about accelerating Your Average, getting out of your box quicker and onto your dreams.

CHAPTER 5

STAYING MOTIVATED

The next thing you'll need to know is how to stay motivated.

It's easier to improve your life from movement than from standing still. You have to create change. To do that, you're going to need some motivation. Because I bet the whole time you've been reading this book you've been thinking to yourself:

> *I get all this, but I'm not good at consistently doing the things that are difficult for me. That's why my bullseye is so small. I have so many negotiables in my life because I'm not good at those things. And I have my Support Wall, my Dream Wall, my Identity Wall and my Relationship Wall to remind me of it! I get that I'm in my box, but my box feels pretty safe most days.*

Well Average Sucks and that's why you're reading this book, so keep reading.

Motivation is one of those words that most people think means to be "fired up." It means to be excited. It means gearing up to do a powerful thing, something big. Motivation, however, is much simpler: motivation is doing something, whether that's what you want to be doing or not.

And as I frequently say, *The World Rewards Those in Motion.*

This is common sense. If you look at your desk and know it's a mess and you need to clean it, you'll get it done if it matters to you. My desk is a mess most of the time because I don't really care about cleaning it, the mess doesn't keep me from taking action.

But when something matters to you and you know you need to get it done, every time you're *not* doing it, you're just spinning your wheels, wasting time and energy. Your life is much more effective once you do what you need to do. After you clean your desk, or make that important call, or send that email, are you exhausted and tired? Nope, you feel energized.

Momentum begets momentum.

When you take action, your brain turns on and your brain automatically says, "What else can I do?" Once you do something, you wind up with more energy to get other things done because there's less of a burden on you. When you get the little things done, you have more room for the big things—but it's the little things that make a difference.

So let's look at what matters.

Let's do a little exercise right now, grab a piece of paper and you can see for yourself how this works.

First, I want you to make a list of four things you need to do.

For now, we'll just focus on number one to get started.

Next, write down something in your life that you have trouble being consistent about—something that really matters, not little things like cleaning your desk or organizing your garage. Something important.

You might say, "I have trouble consistently eating healthy foods." Or "I can't get myself to exercise consistently."

OK hold on to that piece of paper for a minute, I'm going to explain how your brain works when it looks at that list.

The things you need to do on your list are not the real issue, I'm sure you know that. The issue is Your Average.

If you have a problem eating the right foods or exercising regularly, that's not your real problem. I believe you don't take your health seriously, that's the real problem.

If Your Average was a person that valued their health, would you have to worry about eating healthy food? Would you have to make an effort to take care of yourself; think about working out, taking your supplements, sleeping well, paying attention to what your body is telling you?

No, you would do it automatically.

I'll say that again. Whatever your issue is, you don't value it, you don't take it seriously, because if you did, you'd solve it. You'd resolve it and raise Your Average.

If you want to make your health, or your business, or your relationship do what it needs to do, you have to take it seriously because if you don't, you don't get the results you want. You have to make it *matter*.

And when you do that, momentum is created, motivation stays on track and you keep working on those wants. You steadily increase Your Average. And that's exactly where you want to be.

Now, let's get back to your list and figure out what's keeping you from tackling your list, and how to be motivated to get the four things completed and then of course, keep going.

THE ADVANTAGE GAME

You've probably heard of the Pain vs. Pleasure strategy, it's a common old school coaching strategy used to get people to understand what truly drives them. It definitely works. Basically it runs on the principle that 97 percent of the world is motivated by running away from things they don't want, and only 3 percent runs toward the things they want. Only 3 percent of the people in the world are wired to run towards success! Chances are you're in the 97 percent, so pay attention:

I'm going to take this a step further and make sure you understand the underlying psychology that prevents the 97 percent from tackling their list (and keeps you from getting what you want).

Your brain is playing a game of Advantages.

In the simplest terms, your brain has one very important function: to keep you alive. At an even deeper level, you'll realize that your brain is constantly scanning for advantages.

Your brain is constantly looking for ways to feel better, to enjoy more, to be happier. It's working with the chemistry of your body to bring you joy and amazing levels of dopamine and norepinephrine and serotonin.

It's searching for ways to bring you love and happiness and everything else that makes you feel great.

Get this, while your brain is scanning for advantages, it's running a nifty little program called avoidance. Any time your brain sees something that seems difficult, uncomfortable, strange or possibly threatening, it avoids it.

Are you getting this?

I'll summarize: your brain looks for ways to keep you happy and safe and avoids anything it doesn't know with certainty to be good for you.

Let's pretend you have eating healthy as #1 on your list. Let's play this out.

You have to make healthy eating something your brain scans for and declares it an advantage.

Your brain's looking for ways to keep you happy. Ice cream makes you happy! A burger makes you happy! A salad doesn't, unless it's dripping in dressing, maybe then it's not too bad. Do you see why you're having such a challenge? Chocolate, happy! An apple, well, only if there's no chocolate available.

You say you want to eat healthy yet every time you go to pack a salad and veggies for lunch, your brain sets off all these alarms that unconsciously say "Avoid that crappy food that doesn't taste good!" and so you go to work, eat your salad and feel deprived all day. You go home and have a little treat to reward yourself for being good, and your brain says "Yay, happy!" and then triggers you to eat something else unhealthy and you go to bed feeling bad about your food choices. And then the next day you start all over again.

Most people can't stand the idea that they're not where they want to be. They don't realize that their discomfort and frustration are actually a guide to get them where they want to go.

Most people look at discomfort as a bad thing and let their brain run the avoidance program and stay away from what will get them what they want.

So now think of someone you know that is a healthy eater. This person has changed their perception and told their brain that healthy food is good, makes them feel happy and healthy, safe and alive.

Now, think all the way back to the beginning of this book when we talked about change. Remember we said change can come in an instant or with repetition.

I'll show you how that works with this example, and yes it can be super easy when you understand how your brain works, use the message it's sending to motivate you and keep you on track!

For the instant change to the way you eat, something dramatic would have to happen that would create a peak emotional experience. For example:

Imagine it's a beautiful sunny day and you're sitting outside at a new restaurant in town that's got a great vibe, great food and great music. You're having fun chatting away with your friend, simply enjoying the moment and eating a nice healthy salad, when you notice Brad Pitt walking across the room toward your table.

Now it just so happens you think Brad Pitt is the hottest man on the planet (or the biggest badass from *Fight Club*). Your heart races and as he passes your table you make eye contact and give him a smile. He slows down, scans your table, looks up and scans your face and says, "That salad is the best, I order it every time I come here—it's so healthy and delicious!" He smiles again and walks away.

Chances are you're going to want that salad, or one like it, a lot more frequently and never think of it as a punishment or deprivation again. Having Brad Pitt compliment you on your healthy eating choice would definitely be a peak emotional experience. You are forever changed and love eating salad and any veggie for that matter.

Now, for change brought about by repetition, you have to repeat the behavior until it becomes something your brain likes. Truthfully, you could learn to love raw veggies as much as you love chocolate. You make a decision to eat veggies, and you pay attention to how great you felt from doing so, and then repeat. I always say you're not brainwashing yourself, you're washing your brain of old behaviors with repetition. Eat healthy, feel good, notice you feel good, talk to yourself about how good you feel, repeat, repeat, repeat and it will become your new normal, Your Average, your non-negotiable.

I'll give you another interesting example, this time of your brain playing an avoidance game. Let's say you want more money. You might ask, "Why don't I have more money?"

My answer? You can't have it yet, and you don't actually want it.

Immediately you think, "What do you mean I don't want

it? Of course I want it! I'm stressed out of my mind about my finances."

Let's look at how that shows up inside of your brain. You say, "I want more money." Your brain says, "Sounds great! But don't we already have enough money?" Then it thinks, "Well, I don't have enough money because I've screwed up before. I've made some mistakes. I'm not that good with money." And you start to feel insecure.

When you admit that you don't have enough money, that's uncomfortable—and nobody likes to be uncomfortable. It's a lot easier to go spend more than it is to admit that your bank account isn't where you want it to be. It's easier to do whatever you want to do, to avoid what needs to get done.

THE AVOIDANCE GAME

OK, back to your list. Now we'll focus on your brain avoiding things that aren't good for you. In order to create a new automatic program for your brain to follow, we have to change whatever avoidance behavior you're currently doing from good to *bad*.

This is going to require you thinking at a deeper level. Right now, ask yourself the question, "What do I do instead of doing what I need to do?" You must answer this, it's critical to you beating the avoidance game. Write it down.

A lot of what you do is positive. You work, you make money, it keeps you busy and seems productive. Write it down. Are you going to networking meetings, watching Netflix, scrolling through social media, talking with clients—what do you do instead of the things on your list?

Maybe it's reading, creating webinars, going out to eat, or hanging out with friends and family. It could be helping your kids with their homework. There's nothing wrong with that; write it down.

I have a client named John who came to me for help growing his business. He's a fitness coach and wants to grow, expand, make more money and have more clients. By now, we all get that if he wants to grow his business, he needs to take his business seriously.

When I asked what he does instead of what he needs to do, he told me, "I do all the important things that are mandatory; I talk to my clients, I work on social media and I work out—and that takes up all my time."

I asked him how much he talks to his current clients outside of the normal time allotted for a coaching session. He admitted that he often spent more time than necessary chatting with them, even though those clients are the ones that were following the program consistently and getting results. He was talking to his happy customers and calling it work! When I asked him why he was spending extra time with customers that he was already giving great service to, he said, "Because it makes me feei accomplished. I know how to talk to them, so it's easy to keep them happy."

Compared to talking to new people and trying to convince them to hire him, this was a lot easier. "You have two options, buddy," I told him. "You can talk to new people and feel that insecurity and use it to force you to grow, improve your communication and get better at sales or you can talk only to the people you already know, which won't put another dime in your pocket."

Which would you pick? Being insecure or creating more business?

Most people would pick their comfort zone and stay in their box.

Logically you'd think you would pound the pavement looking for more clients, but logically you'd eat that salad, too. And that's not what most people *actually* do.

That's not how the majority of people in this world behave.

I wouldn't have built the coaching business I have if I didn't understand that emotions drive people, not logic. Even the most analytical people in the world are driven by emotion.

I don't want you to solve this; I want you to understand and respect that below the surface, your brain is laying out your options. You can either talk to people who already like you and are happy with you, who make you feel good, or you can explain yourself and hope people believe in your value enough to take money out of their pocket and hand it over to you. I'm not saying you're stuck here, I simply want you to understand yourself so you can outsmart the Avoidance program.

We all like feeling positive so much that we willingly trade out the things we should be doing for the things that feel good.

On your list of things you are doing instead of focusing on your wants, what can you eliminate? Could you spend less time on social media under the guise of "it's work?" Could you get a really great workout in an hour as opposed to ninety minutes and free up thirty minutes to book a conference call with a prospect? Could you say no to Netflix and spend an hour writing out an email campaign to market your product? You get the idea.

You love results. Your brain gets off on results. Here's the problem, if you're not getting the right results you still go to bed at night pissed off at yourself because you didn't do what you needed to do. You don't like it that Your Average Sucks.

TRICKING YOUR BRAIN

Here's another strategy you'll want to start using right away to ignore your Walls, raise your Average, and get out of your box.

It's called a Trigger Word.

First, ask yourself, "What's the worst-case scenario if I don't change?" What is the absolute worst thing that can and will happen if I don't take action?

Then, find a word that summarizes that worst-case scenario and reminds you of what will happen if you don't do what you need to do and become who you want to be.

You have to find a highly impactful word that moves you. It's got to make you mad and make you feel a gut-punch. A Trigger Word reminds you of the pain you will feel if you don't do what needs to get done. If that word doesn't move you, if you don't feel it viscerally, it won't work.

You'll want to make a billboard out of that Trigger Word in your mind and every time you find yourself avoiding an action, think of that word. It'll trigger you to get you moving into gear faster than a speeding bullet. I have clients that print out their Trigger Word in big huge font and tape the paper anywhere they need to remind themselves to push past the avoidance. If they want to eat healthy and have a weakness for snacks, they stick it in their pantry or in the fridge. If they talk themselves out of exercising, they put it right by their sneakers.

In their office, by the phone, I've even had some people tell me they make their Trigger Word their screen saver as a constant reminder! Another tip I give when people are deciding on their Trigger Word is to run it by this test: Would you wear it on a shirt? As a woman you might wear a shirt that says "Bitch," but I doubt you'd wear a shirt that says "Fraud," "Liar," or "Hypocrite."

Example: One of my first clients ever was a guy named Jeremy. Jeremy wanted to lose a significant amount of weight. He was a has-been college basketball star, but that was thirty years and a hundred pounds ago. He had a beautiful wife—a yoga instructor—and three healthy children. He didn't have any glandular problems or mental health or abuse issues that would prevent him from losing weight. He did, however, have a little too much fun going with his friends to watch Thursday night football with beer and nachos.

Jeremy's list of "what I do instead of going to the gym" was a packed schedule of social activities; barbeques, happy hours, pizza with the kids, you name it.

So then I asked him, "What happened the last time you went to exercise?"

He remembered exactly: "December twenty-third last year, I was getting ready to go to a holiday party and looked in the mirror and saw nothing but fat. I don't look at myself much, but this was a formal party and I had to put on a tux and well...mine didn't fit. I was trying to button the pants and couldn't and when I finally took a good look in the mirror, it was not good. I had to squeeze into that tux and was miserable all night so right there and then I decided I was going to get myself in better shape. Since it was the holidays, I made it my resolution: I would start in the New Year. What would a few more days of fat matter, I couldn't change anything that quickly anyway so might as well enjoy myself over Christmas. On January first, I woke up with a terrible hangover, so I decided to start on the second. And I did it! I got up on January second, and I went to the gym.

"I used to have a membership there but my credit card

had expired and I'd ignored the billing notices, but hadn't canceled my membership. So when I walked in I owed them almost two years of back dues, almost $5,000. I could have walked away and not paid for it, but I had committed to working out that day, and I had the money, so I updated my credit card and went in. I went into the locker room to change which was horribly embarrassing. Everyone was in better shape than I was, by a lot. The gym was totally rearranged since the last time I was there and had all kinds of new equipment I didn't know how to use. I couldn't lift much weight, and my body felt heavy and sluggish on the cardio machines. I was sweating, and not the look-at-me-I'm-Hercules kind of sweat. I was sweating so much it was disgusting and I had to wipe down every machine I used because it was soaked. I hated it.

"When I left I did walk out proud that at least I'd made the effort. But then when I got to the car I checked my phone and I had three missed messages. In that one hour at the gym, I'd missed my kids asking me to go play mini golf because they had a day off of school, my boss called because he needed me to do something and my wife called to make sure I took the kids to mini golf. My day hadn't even started and I was already sweaty, sore, uncomfortable and guilty."

"You see why happy hour sounds a lot better than that?"

He nodded.

So then I asked him, "What's the worst-case scenario if you never lose weight?"

"Well," he replied, "I could have a heart attack."

"OK," I said, "what if you have a heart attack, have a bypass, and still don't change?"

"Well, I could die," he said very quietly.

"Well, we're all dying. Everyone's dying from a terminal illness, called birth. That's not unique to you, we all live with that. What else?"

He stared at me blankly. I knew he was wondering what could be worse than death. So I drew him a picture of how I, objectively, saw his worst case. I knew that his wife did yoga all the time and was super healthy. So I asked him, "What if one day you walk in the door and your wife sits you down for a BIG TALK and explains that all these years of you not taking care of yourself has paid the toll, and she's tired of it, no longer attracted to you, and doesn't even know if she loves you anymore?"

He was shell shocked.

So then I went on, really wanting to drive home the point.

"What about your children? You tell them to eat their vegetables at dinner, right?"

"Sure, I do," he says.

Well, you and I both know that Jeremy can tell his kids to be healthy all day, but if they see him eating whatever he wants and never exercising, they are watching. To make certain he got the point, I reminded him of the lesson he's teaching his kids and the outcome he's bound to experience.

"Your kids will either grow up just like you; they'll have bad habits, be fat, teased, insecure and die young, or they will be healthy and resent you and be embarrassed of you.

"And if you do die young," I told him, "you'll miss their games, their graduations, and their weddings. That's pretty selfish. Do you really want to teach your kids how to die young? You're out of integrity with yourself, and you're setting a horrible example for your kids."

As you can see, I'm not here to make you feel good. Yet I do want you to feel *something*.

He got the message and right then and there set his Trigger Word as "**bad dad**." For the first little while, he said it to himself any time his Old Average tried to talk him out of exercising or eating healthy. Fast-forward, I can tell you that today Jeremy is healthy. Being healthy is now a non-negotiable for him, and he and his wife enjoy the same health and are on the same page.

Now, go back to your list.

Imagine if every time you went for it, you used your Trigger Word to keep you going. Your Trigger Word has so much power. It will allow you to shut out the walls that keep you Average and keep you in your box.

Imagine how fast you'll accomplish your list!

Imagine how quickly you'll move your wants and dreams into your bullseye!

Imagine how quickly you'll Raise Your Average.

CHAPTER 6

RAISE YOUR AVERAGE

Up until this point we've been laying the groundwork for Raising Your Average. You understand where you are, how you got there, where you're going and how to get there. You're on your way to getting out of the box to a New Average.

This chapter is going to show you how to approach the changes you must make.

As you read through this chapter, you're going to find many tools and strategies that will make being consistent easier than you've ever experienced in your life.

MINIMUM ACTION PROGRESS PLAN

You're going to love this next section you're about to read. It'll allow you to breathe a sigh of relief. Because when most people hear it's time to "Raise Your Average" they immediately think they're going to have to work even harder. That can't be farther from the truth. First of all, your life is about to get much easier because a) You're being yourself and b) You're going to get really good at living your life.

It's called the Minimum Action Progress Plan.

I know it sounds like I'm suggesting you take the easy road, but that's not it.

It may seem like it should be easy to change Your Average; you just have to work hard and push through until you make it. That's not it, either. Even though I'm guessing that your entire childhood your parents, teachers and coaches probably told you the same thing mine told me: work hard, be a good person, do the right thing, and you'll get there.

That's the absolute *worst* advice. You can work hard, keep working hard, and it still isn't enough and eventually all you end up with is frustration and burnout.

And, by the way, everyone knows that crash diets and

rapid weight loss end up in people gaining back the weight, this time with a slower metabolism and a bigger battle.

And we've all heard about people who won the lottery and ended up bankrupt just a few years later.

The whole personal development movement, especially in the 1980s and 90s, was all about massive action. It's about pushing yourself to get what you want as quickly as possible. If you just work hard and get where you want to go quickly, it will all work out.

Today the buzz word is *hustle*. I am not a fan.

You've probably burned out in the past. And you remember what happened, you lost motivation and you lost momentum and you had to start all over again and scratch and claw your way back out of the box. The problem is that, typically, you're not going to make it stick by only trying harder.

The key to making it stick in our life is counterintuitive.

With the Minimum Action Progress Plan, you don't go from 0 to 100. You figure out where you're starting from, and you take the smallest step necessary to make progress. You go from level one to level two. Then, once level two has become your new average, you step up to level three.

Eventually, step by step by step, you make it to 100 and out of the box. Progress is made and Your Average is reset in small steps, not giant leaps.

In 2004, a guy named Andy called me on the phone and asked me to coach him. He was famous in his niche and was ready for his next big part. "Michael, I want to land this movie role playing a Spartan. Think like the movie *300*."

If you remember what those Spartans look like, they were in amazing shape. Not a single one of them had an "average" body. Andy had some work to do—and he only had six months to do it.

I asked him what his plan was, and—oh boy—he had a good one. It involved working out three times a day—cardio in the morning, yoga in the afternoon, and weight training at night—six days a week, and swimming or doing push-ups on his "rest" day. He was also going to eat five healthy meals every day, seven days a week, and no going out to eat.

"That's awesome," I told him. "But how often do you work out now? How often do you already eat healthy meals?"

"Well," he said, "I go to the gym about three or four days a week. And most days, I eat a couple of healthy meals, but I go out to eat a few times a week."

Andy wasn't going from 0 to 100, but eating a couple of healthy meals a day, five or six days a week—ten or twelve meals total—is a big jump to eating thirty-five healthy meals a week. Similarly, working out three times a week is a far cry from working out three times a *day*.

And I told him as much.

"That's my secret," Andy said proudly. "Six months of massive action!"

I had to ask him, "Are you looking for massive action, which also leads to massive burnout? Or are you looking to get the part in the movie and create a new average for yourself? If it's the first, great! You've got a plan for that. But if you really want that part, I'm going to recommend a process that will get you what you want—yet you have to follow my instructions exactly."

"Great, I'm in," he said. "What do I have to do?"

I gave Andy his first assignment in the Minimum Action Progress Plan. "I want you to eat as many healthy meals as you can eat for the next seven days. No minimum, no maximum, just write them down and let me know how many you did."

"What about working out?" he asked.

"Don't even worry about it. Let's just do the food this week."

"But that will set me back! I'll be even further behind if I don't make the most of every week for the next six months!"

"Just the food," I said.

Seven days later we talked. "Andy, how was your week?"

He answered, "Great...I think."

"How many healthy meals did you eat?"

"About sixteen."

"OK. I know you wanted to get to thirty-five, so that's about halfway there. That's a good start! Did you work out?"

Almost guiltily, he replied, "Yeah, five times."

"That's great! You worked out almost every day this week."

"OK," he said. "Can I go full speed now?"

> "Let's do one more week of the same plan. Let me know how many healthy meals you eat and how often you work out, if you do."

We met again the following week, and Andy was ready with his answers right away: "I ate twenty-one healthy meals—more than last week—and I worked out six times, one more than the week before. Can I start my plan now? I really gotta turn this on, man."

I asked him to do one more week—it takes twenty-one days to build a habit, after all—and report back. He agreed.

> "All right, Michael. I had twenty-four healthy meals and worked out six times."
>
> "Congratulations!" I said.
>
> "Why are you congratulating me? I haven't hit my goal."
>
> "I'm saying congratulations," I said, "because we officially know your baseline. We learned Your Average, so we knew where to start. And you've been making progress ever since, slowly changing Your Average instead of jumping in then giving up."

Andy thought about that for a moment and then said, "You know what? I will never go back to where I was again."

And since that day, he hasn't.

He wound up getting the part in the movie, but more importantly, he reset where he is. He never works out fewer than five days a week, because he built that new standard for himself.

Do you see how that works? You want to get from point A to point B, but if you burn out it'll take you even longer to get there. When you take steady, incremental and progressive action, you will get there. You'll be consistent, have momentum working in your favor and a lot less stress on your mind and body.

That was the beginning of Andy's new average, and today is the beginning of yours.

A GLOBAL PERSPECTIVE

Now we're going to move on to create an approach to raising Your Average. With any activity in life, I encourage people to take a global perspective and look at the entire picture before making a move.

The Global Perspective allows you to disassociate or disconnect from the emotion connected with whatever you're trying to accomplish. When you can be objective about Your Average you'll be able to identify the actions you must take, stay motivated to take those actions, get out of your box and Raise Your Average.

What we're going to do now is ask three simple questions that will give you a global perspective of your Current Average. The answers to these questions will help Raise Your Average in an effective way and accelerate what you're doing.

QUESTION 1—IF AN OUTSIDER LOOKED AT THE WAY YOU LIVE, HOW WOULD THEY DESCRIBE WHAT YOU DO?

I don't know how it is at your house, but for most people, we don't like hearing what we should be doing from the people who know us the best. Certainly I don't love it when my wife points out the obvious, nope not at all, even if she's right.

And on the flip side—she's not thrilled when I make a small suggestion for an improvement I see but she apparently hadn't yet. Same thing goes for my teenager, she'll definitely get irritated if we try to tell her what, when or how she should do something. I'm sure you're chuckling as you read this, because we all know what it feels like to be on both ends of that stick. It's not all that effective.

So let's go ask someone else. Imagine you hired a consultant, someone you paid a lot of money to come in and take a look at your life. They'd observe everything you did that contributes to your Current Average. Visualize them following you for a couple of weeks watching every move (well *almost* every move). They would watch your activities, see what clothes you wear, what you eat, how you treat people, how others treat you, how you spend money, how hard you work, how much you *didn't* work—everything you do over two weeks.

So for today, I want you to pretend you hired yourself as a consultant. Now take a step back and take a good look at everything you're doing.

My first question for you is, "If an outsider was looking at how you live, how would they describe what you do?"

Professionally, they probably wouldn't beat you up, but they would tell it like it is. They're not going to say you're lazy or stupid—you reserve that for yourself, so your brain can keep you where you are—but they will be completely honest.

For years, if an outside consultant would have watched me, they would have said, "Michael, you have a lot of potential, but you're unorganized. You make projects—like writing this book—way more complicated than they need to be. You don't let people help you as much as you should, and you're playing smaller than you should be playing."

Then they would say, "In order to get where you want to go, you need to change some things. Here's a list."

So imagine an outsider looked at you. Imagine they take a look at your life, your health, your relationships, your finances. What would they say about you? You'd be totally exposed, which would give you the answers you need—the honest answers, of course—on the areas you need to focus on to Raise Your Average.

You'd have an actual list of what you needed to do. And I guarantee you if you compare that list to the score you gave yourself in the Average Assessment a couple of chapters back, it would all fit together.

It's very important to know this, but the second question will lead to even more.

QUESTION 2—WHAT WAS YOUR ORIGINAL REASON FOR DOING WHAT YOU DO?

I want you to remember learning how to ride a bike. (If you don't know how, I want you to *imagine* learning how.) When you were a kid, before you ever rode a bike, why did you want to?

For me, I wanted to ride that bike because it was a challenge. I saw a lot of people riding their bikes all around my neighborhood in White Meadow Lake, New Jersey, and I wanted to join them! I'd see a kid riding by my house with a big smile and the wind blowing their hair and I knew I wanted in on that. When my dad set out to teach me how to ride, I learned quickly because I was determined to get it. After that I had freedom and my friends and I went all over the place. It was a good time. Eventually I used the bike as transportation to take me to Domenico's Pizza where I worked during high school. Now, as an adult, I ride a bike for exercise. My reasons have changed over time.

And that brings us to my second question for you: "what was your original reason for doing what you do?"

In my thirties I had trouble getting myself to work out. I couldn't figure out why. I had been an athlete as a teenager, through high school and college. I knew how to work out then. I couldn't *wait* to start lifting weights when I turned thirteen. Hockey is a serious cardio workout, and I played for years, and went to the gym on top of that. And here I was at thirty, a little overweight, not taking care of myself.

I thought, "What's going on? You can afford to hire a trainer. Why aren't you working out?"

And then I asked myself this second question. "What was my original reason for working out?"

Well, when I was thirteen, I wanted to be in great shape for playing ice hockey. I wanted to impress girls. I wanted to be able to defend myself if I ever got in a fight. And I was part of a team, so we all worked out together.

That answer gave me some big reasons why I was having trouble working out. I wasn't on a team anymore; I played here and there. I'd already impressed a girl enough to marry me, so that base was covered. If I got into a fight as an adult, I'd go to jail, and I'm not the fighting type anyway, I'd much rather talk it out.

Let's look at this from another angle: my business.

If an outsider looked at how I run my business, he would see me as unorganized and capable of more but not getting what I want. My original reason for going into business was to survive. I needed to pay my bills. I also wanted to prove that I could build my own business and not have a JOB like everyone thought you were supposed to do after college. And of course, I wanted to pick a career where I could truly help people, enjoy my work and truthfully—feel good about myself.

After ten years in business—after doing millions of dollars

of business a year—I was still making decisions based on survival. And I still wasn't getting what I wanted.

Then I had a realization: I had already survived. I had proven my point. I was helping people on a regular basis. I was doing exactly what I wanted, but I hadn't consciously raised My Average.

So let's put this in the perspective of My Average. I'd moved all these things on my want and dream list to my non-negotiable bullseye. Day in and day out I was living my dreams. What I wanted ten years ago was now my normal. It was incredible, yet I did what most people do, and forgot to reset my target. My Average had gone up in all types of areas, but I was still grinding in survival mode, which kept My Average lower than it needed to be.

And that brings us to the final question.

QUESTION 3—WHAT WILL IT LOOK LIKE WHEN YOU'VE ALREADY ACHIEVED WHAT YOU WANT?

If you're already doing what you want to be doing—when the moment comes when you are living your wants and dreams, what would you make your life about? What would you make your career or your business about?

You are already doing a lot of the things you *want* to be

doing. If you stand in the possibility that you're already making a lot of what you want to happen in this world, what would your plan be from here?

Once you have a New Average, what will be next? I asked myself this question a couple of years ago and when I did, it changed everything for me. When I stood in the possibility that I had already achieved my goals, I started redirecting the target of my business. Instead of survival, my original business plan, I improved my plan that said, "Why not help people and build a profitable company that makes a difference in the world?"

That's a much bigger step and I definitely leveled up My Average.

Accepting my own influence in the world was a seriously powerful way of looking at it.

I chose to take on the responsibility, to not just build a company, yet to show the world how to solve the majority of their challenges through communication.

Now ask yourself that same question. What will your life be about next? Maybe it is Oprah endorsing your book or being a guest on Dr. Oz or playing in the NHL. What would that New Average look like for you?

Your brain will always try to drive you back to your old average. There is no more dominating force in your life than the desire to remain in your current average.

Raising Your Average is about deleting what *was* and building what *is*, in order to get what you want.

Now that you have this overview of yourself, this global perspective of Your Average, you can work on changing the specific things keeping you in your box.

THE FORMULA FOR CHANGE BY REPETITION

All through this book we've talked about making the changes necessary to raise Your Average. We've talked about the two types of change, instant and through repetition.

You also have your list of the first four things you want in your life. And I'm sure you can make a list of the specific tasks or actions required for you to achieve them.

So you should be set, right? You can put this book down and get to work.

However, you're going to need a bit more help with the change through repetition. Remember that Adversity that we're going to use to your advantage? It's going to happen, and you now know that it's a good thing, yet I'd be omitting one of the most important factors of success if I got you all fired up to raise Your Average and didn't give you a specific strategy for the times when you come up against Adversity. I want to be sure that you know how to handle any of your four walls that try to keep you where you're at.

If you study marketing or sales of any kind, you know there is always a strategy to people's habits and buying patterns. A good marketer will look for those patterns and then build their whole campaign around those patterns, ensuring that they put the right message in front of the buyer at the right time, in the right place, with the right emotion. This is how I help people build their sales presentations, and how you can approach your own actions.

This formula hits on every element you and your brain need to Raise Your Average.

RECENCY + FREQUENCY + DURATION + INTENSITY = CONVERSION

Take a look at the actions you must take. You want to take your *wants* and move them to Your Average, and ultimately move your *dreams* to Your Average. The fastest way to make the changes to your behavior permanent (non-negotiable) is to understand and live by this formula.

If you've ever been to Disney and stood in line for hours to get on Space Mountain, you know what the slow line is like...painful, but you want the result so you're willing to pay the price of your time. Then when you discover "Fast-Pass" and you think that's the greatest thing because you can shortcut one ride at a time. That's nice, less standing in line. Then Disney came up with "MaxPass," which is even better because you can use your phone to get an even better shortcut and now you can ride even more rides and spend even less time standing in lines! This means you'll have a lot more fun at Disney. Great. We've taken our girls to Disney a bunch of times and been able to ride more rides because of these Disney benefits. But then, my friend Kent told me about this private tour you could buy that came with your very own tour guide who took you through the park all day and FastPassed you to the front of every ride, giving you front row reserved seats to all the parades and fireworks and, well...I was all over that. Best way to do Disney, hands down.

This formula for change is like that. It's a huge shortcut and it works based on how your brain works, so it works. It will be incredibly helpful to you as you go through your days; your Trigger words will get you going and then you'll apply these principles to make the change stick. Point blank you'll get more done in less time.

RECENCY

Let's say you want to get in better shape. Most people say, "I'm going to work out every day for the rest of my life," or, "I'll start going to the gym on Monday."

Your brain's already heard you say this before, so it knows that you're just going to quit in two weeks anyway.

Yet if you do something recently, your brain is much more familiar with it and sees it as safe.

Remember Jeremy whose most recent visit to the gym was two years prior? His brain didn't have anything recent or familiar to rely on to send him a message saying, "Great idea, let's go!" Instead his brain said, "We haven't done this in a very long time, that must be a bad sign, this isn't a great idea."

Great, you say, but how do I go to the gym more, because that's my problem?

Here's a trick. At my office our team says **decide and do**. And we master that mantra by making small commitments.

Why not trick your brain by saying something simple? "I'll work out for the next two days." You only have to do it Monday and Tuesday, and start sending the recency signals to the brain. Since we know that momentum begets momentum, watch what happens. Once you go Monday and Tuesday, you'll start planning for Wednesday and Thursday, or maybe even Thursday and Friday, yet the commitment is there, the recency is there, and a new behavior is being formed.

Bottom line, you want the behavior to be familiar to the brain and recency will make that happen. This creates a new neural pathway. When you've had an experience doing something before, it's always easier the second time around. That's what neural pathways are about.

This is why you can take $1 million away from a successful person and they'll get it back quickly, or why someone in phenomenal shape can bounce back faster than someone who's never worked out before.

FREQUENCY

This refers to how often an event occurs. This is simply repetition and the clearest message you can send to your brain. This is where "21 Days to Create a Habit" comes from. Do something over and over again and it becomes Your Average. It also creates "Unconscious Competence" which is being really good at something without having to think about it. Driving is the perfect example. When you're learning how to drive you pay attention to every single thing that's happening, but once you learn how, you just get in the car and drive. Frequency created a habit.

Frequency with exercise, that's an easy one to figure out. Go for a run, even for a single mile, every day, will create a runner out of you.

Now let's talk about how a smoker starts smoking, or a smoker quits smoking. It works the same either way.

You smoke a cigarette for the first time and you cough and your throat burns and it smells bad. You felt relaxed or got a little buzz from it and you remember that but the bad taste makes you think twice about smoking again. But there you are one day and the situation is just right and you light up another. Same thing, burn, cough, smell, buzz. The more frequently you do it, the more the nicotine has a chance to get a hold on you and create an addiction, and boom...you're a smoker. It wasn't the individual cigarette and it wasn't the nicotine that made you the smoker—it was the frequency.

Quitting smoking is the same in reverse...get frequency on your side. Not quite as easy because now you have nicotine working against you, but it can be done. You smoke, but then one day you don't, it's not easy but you went a whole day.

Then the next day you keep yourself busy all day and manage to make it day two smoke free.

Third day, no cigarettes.

You're super proud of yourself and even though you're jittery you realize in your mind that the frequency of you NOT smoking is working in your favor. Keep it up, keep up the frequency of you being a person that's healthy and values your lungs and your life, and you'll be able to let your brain know that you don't smoke.

Knowing how the brain works and why you must be consistent will definitely reduce the temptation you may have to do or not do something, and make the change stick much sooner.

Can you feel Your Average increasing?

DURATION

The first time you do anything is the hardest.

The first time I did a Spartan Race was definitely a huge challenge for me. I wasn't in Spartan condition when I started training, by any means. I trained hard to make sure I was in primo condition and all I wanted to do was make it through the race. Sure I wanted a good time and

I wanted to complete each obstacle, but I was going with my Minimal Action Progress Plan and my perspective was set to do well without burning out or getting injured.

While I was training there was one thing I could not master, and that was the grip. There are several obstacles which require you to hang, pull yourself up on a rope, go across monkey bars and ring a bell, etc. (and remember, I have an Identity Wall from my past that says I'm a guy that can't do pull-ups telling me I'm not able to do it). I knew that getting through this race required grip strength and so I practiced, all the time—getting in my recency and frequency.

But I also did something that made a huge difference and worked on my duration. I'd go to adult open gym at Scottsdale Gymnastics, where both of my daughters have gone for many years, and practice hanging as long as I could. I'd climb the rope and hang on to it, extending my duration each time.

That's what got me through the Spartan Race. I'd sent a message to my brain over and over that said, I can grip something and hang my body weight from it for a long period of time. My brain converted that to "hanging on for dear life is easy." OK, maybe not easy, but doable!

For you, what if you set your mind to push a little longer

the next time you're doing something? Five more minutes on the treadmill, one more cold call to a prospect, an extra text to your family, it will add up in your favor.

INTENSITY

Intensity is how intense the experience really is; how significant the emotional feeling is that's attached to the behavior.

For a minute, let's go back to the peak emotional experience that brings about instant change. A peak emotional experience is full of intense emotions, positive or negative. The intensity is so high that it invokes change.

I once had a lady that was held hostage on a bus. There were some very bad men in black masks with guns that jumped on the bus and held everyone hostage for two hours. She was traumatized, and even though she was in her mid-40s, which means she had lived over 394,000 hours on this earth, those two hours built four solid walls and destroyed her Average for a very long time. The intensity of those two hours changed her, which is why she was at my event. She wanted to make a change and be free from her box, which is what we did—we changed her perceptions which freed her mind up to move on and create a New Average, which gave her the ability to live a normal life, doing normal day-to-day activities as if she'd never stepped on that bus. She's got a New Average.

So how do you create intensity in normal everyday situations? Well, you can plan to eat lunch at the same restaurant as Brad Pitt, which would be odd, or you could look for ways to add intensity to your actions.

Here's an example, you want to work on your marriage because you're in a rut. Life got busy and the focus shifted from the love between the two of you to your adult responsibilities. You work long hours at your job, pay your bills, spend time with your kids and take your Basset Hound for walks in the evening. The last person on your list is the love of your life, how bizarre is that!

So...you want to make an effort so you make plans to go out on a date, but it seems like you can't find anything to talk about besides the kids. You are also tired all the time from all these responsibilities so after dinner you just want to go home and go to bed. There's absolutely no intensity whatsoever, and although you can remember all the fun and hot nights you used to have, there's no conjuring up the strength to recreate that again anytime soon. How could you add intensity to fixing your relationship? You'll have to go to extremes.

Why not go for a surprise and rent a hotel room in the

middle of the day for no reason. Show up at their office with lunch. Ask them to go for a run with you.

Do *something* that would take it up a notch and create a little intensity. Have fun! Smile, laugh, feel. It's a great start and will send a message to your brain; this was a new, intense and important experience, even if it was just a couple of hours.

It'll be worth it.

CONVERSION

Conversion is simply the result of everything adding up into one thing. 1+1=2. Conversion goes on all around you, without you even realizing it.

The brain is constantly converting the messages you send it into the programs it runs automatically.

If you've recently been exercising all the time and someone tells you how great you look, you've nailed recency, frequency and intensity. That converts to a change.

If you spend all your free time over the last two months building a new marketing campaign, and you mail it out and make a ton of sales and bring in thousands of dollars in revenue, that converts to a change.

This is how you raise Your Average. You take actions on your wants and dreams. You get out of your box. You love your life.

NOT YOUR AVERAGE FAIL SAFES

My company is called the Human Communications Institute. I selected that name because I understood that every single challenge in life can be resolved with effective communication.

Whether it's you effectively talking to yourself in your own head so you can be mentally and emotionally strong, or it's you speaking with other people in your personal or professional life and able to communicate a message and do it well.

Your future hinges on your ability to effectively communicate.

Here's an example of how subtle shifts in your language can change your mindset. Many people will say their wedding was the greatest day of their entire lives. If that's the greatest thing, what does the future look like? Does that mean everything after that one day is a letdown?

Now, it may have been *one of* the greatest days of their lives *up to that point*. But do you hear how different that sounds? "The greatest day of my entire life" is so powerful and so ridiculous at the same time.

I'm not saying it can't be a great day, but *from a language point of view*, if you say it's the greatest day of your life, every other day is not as good, and that doesn't feel good whatsoever.

As you prepare for the adversity and resistance you're going to encounter, here are a few communication fail safes, aka strategies, that will keep you growing and going.

LANGUAGE PATTERNS

More Often Than Not

Most people fail before they get started because of how they talk about what they are about to do. You can say these four little words to yourself to keep you moving. It's a strategy that's especially useful when you're tempted to bust out of your Minimum Action Progress Plan and risk burnout from massive action. All you have to do is simply say "More Often Than Not" I will...and fill in the blank. My clients *love* this one because it immediately puts their mind at ease. Want to be consistent at working out? Great, instead of saying "My New Year's resolution is to work out five days a week for the entire year," you can simply say "I'm going to exercise more often than not," and stick to that commitment. It'll remove guilt and doing something more often than not is what changes Your Average.

The Category Shift

Right now I'm going to teach you a simple language pattern that is super easy to use.

This strategy raises your awareness of your behaviors and actions and any time you can become more aware, it's easier to make a shift.

I'll demonstrate how it works with an example for healthy eating, which will make a difference in everything you put in your body.

Let's say that you want to lose weight, or maybe just make healthier food choices. With this new pattern, you can eat whatever you want and I can help you lose weight and feel better in the next two weeks. Check this out.

It's not only eating that affects your waistline; it's language. Language affects the nervous system. Language sends messages to your brain.

Let's look at the language we use around food.

People tend to generalize things and lump things

together. We call all the things we eat "food," whether it's a McDonald's hamburger or a nice steak, a potato or a salad, a milkshake or cereal. It's all just *food*. When you lump everything all in one category and you don't qualify the category, your brain doesn't know what to do with it.

This will create a different relationship with your food. If you're going to put something into your body, you should probably know what it is, so I've broken food into three categories:

1. The first category is **nutrition**. Is there a difference between steamed broccoli and broccoli with nacho cheese pumped all over it? Yes. One is nutritious, the other is not.
2. The second category is **entertainment**. Broccoli is nutrition, pizza is entertainment.
3. And that brings us to our third category. One slice of pizza is entertainment, maybe two. But when you sit down and eat the whole pizza—like I did when I used to work at a pizzeria—that is **addiction**.

A little popcorn at the movies? Entertainment. A huge bucket with a refill plus a large Coke? Addiction.

Before you take your first bite, sip, whatever—talk to your food. Ask it questions. Where did you come from? Are you nutrition, are you entertainment, are you addiction?

Using this Category Shift for your food will make it much easier to choose the option that falls under nutrition. You can create a language pattern for almost anything in your life, using it as a fail safe for when you are off track.

The same Category Shift can be applied to work-related tasks. Ask questions! So, Facebook—are you helping me **grow** my business, am I looking for **entertainment** right now, or am I **addicted**? When you find yourself scrolling the news feed all day long and you can't enjoy a special moment because you're already filming and thinking of what text you'll include with your post, you may want to ask yourself if you're feeding your addiction and starving your business.

And of course you can definitely use the Category Shift in your relationships. Let's say you're dating someone and you're not sure if they're a keeper or not. If you are very much interested in finding someone to share the rest of your life with, you'll want to be certain that you're spending your time with someone that could fill that role. Again, ask questions! As you spend time with them, observe their behavior; how they treat you, how honorable they are, how they make you feel, how motivated they are for their future and ask yourself, is this a **commitment** or is this **entertainment**?

Get vs. Have

What would you rather do, *get* your goal or *have* a goal?

As you know, I play hockey. When I go to my games and *get* a goal, I scored. That's what I want. I also *have* a goal—it's a metal frame with a net sitting in my garage that I pull out to play street hockey.

I've recognized that most people get off on *having*, and they don't spend their time *getting*.

Having is a dream board. *Having* a goal is touching it. *Having* is, "Oh, look at my goal. You want to see it? I'm going to have a beach house and a Ferrari, and it's going to be awesome!" "I'm going to be financially free by next year!"

If you don't know how to get what you want but you have a goal, you're just getting off on the idea of having it—and that's what most people do. Studies have been done that show people get just as excited talking about having something as they do actually having it.

I spent years having goals...but I didn't know how to *get* those goals. I used to do goal-setting the way everybody else did: write it down, state it in the positive, go get what you want. That didn't work for me. I never got very far.

The minute I changed my language around my goals to

getting instead of *having* it created a desire in me to take more action, and it will for you, too.

Start here:

As you take steps to Raise Your Average, say to yourself "I will get my New Average."

Try vs. Will

I'm definitely not the first person to say this one, even Yoda said it, however I must include it because it's a quick change you can make that is important and impactful.

I will keep it super brief.

Do not say TRY unless you're sure it's the right word at the right time. TRY is a back out clause and sets you up to fail. You're either going to do it or you're not.

You may do something that doesn't turn out right, and that's OK. You can do it again. Using the word *will* speaks to your commitment to growth.

Easy example: I'll try to be at your party vs. I will be at your party or even I won't be at your party.

I'd much rather have a real solid answer than a vague one.

Using powerful words that keep you committed will help raise Your Average.

These Fail Safes are here to help you gain a new perception of the changes you'll make as you Raise Your Average.

Using these will allow you to be intuitive, creative and prevent you from getting stuck.

Knowing these will give you a nice little advantage as you strategically design Your Average, *and it will simplify the process of change.*

You're done waiting. It's time to go get what you want.

CONCLUSION

YOUR NEW AVERAGE

Congratulations!

You are Above Average because you read this book.

Now remember, with every action—every decision you make, every step you take—you are influencing Your Average. From here it's going to become easier and more automatic so you can get what you want.

And in the process of you creating your New Average, you'll be able to accept the power of your own influence and join me on my mission to impact the world by raising Averages, one person at a time.

Now put this book down and go take action.

ABOUT THE AUTHOR

Michael was born in Rockaway, New Jersey in 1977, where he lived with parents Neil and Sandra, and sister Risa. In the fifth grade when asked to describe his life in advance for a school project he said, "I want to help people and make them feel better." Today if you asked him how long he's been in the business of changing people's lives, he'd smile quietly and tell you his entire life. After high school he headed west to attend Arizona State University where he received a BIS in Communication and Tourism. He made Arizona his permanent home and now lives in Scottsdale with his wife, Debra and two daughters, Tara and Maya.

Michael tapped into his unmatched natural-born talent

and used that as a running head start while he pursued a deep understanding of psychology and human behavior. He went on to found Human Communications Institute in 2005, which is now a leader in the personal and professional development industry. His innate and highly tuned awareness along with decades of research, allows him to quickly perceive what makes people make the decisions they make, and what makes them do what they do. Rather than breaking down walls, Michael is skilled at getting people to rapidly lower resistance in themselves and others, allowing room for progress.

In 2009, Michael developed Human Interaction Technology™ (HIT), a powerful technology that allows people to understand unknown psychological triggers and powerful communication strategies so they can increase their charisma, influence, persuasion, and connections with others. Using this technology, Michael spends the majority of his career coaching people to improve their communication and influence, leading to greater financial wealth, meaningful relationships, physical health, and confidence throughout their day-to-day life. And with this technology, results last...permanently.

You'll often find Michael on the sidelines watching his daughter, Tara, cheer on her team, or at the ice rink either playing recreational hockey or helping his daughter, Maya, tie her skates for figure skating lessons. If not that, he's hanging out with family and friends or he's reading, usually five or six books at the same time.

In 2017 he created his Circle of Influence Mastermind which is a community of people committed to using their communication and influence skills to impact the world.